FamilyLife
presents a

WEEKEND TO REMEMBER™

Special Acknowledgment

FamilyLife owes a debt of gratitude to a special couple whose lives and material helped shape this ministry from its inception. Don and Sally Meredith, president and cofounders respectively of Christian Family Life, Inc., not only gave this ministry a great start, but also an invaluable message for marriage today.

Name *Brenda Chewning-Kulick*

FAMILYLIFE, 5800 Ranch Drive
Little Rock, Arkansas 72223
1-800-FL-TODAY (358-6329), 24 hours a day
www.familylife.com
A division of Campus Crusade for Christ, Inc.

Welcome to the Weekend to Remember!

I congratulate you on your desire to work together to learn about how to build a marriage that will last a lifetime.

What you are about to hear this weekend is not one man's opinion on marriage. Instead, it is the result of more than two decades of biblical research by a team of men and women who distilled what it takes to have a successful marriage and family. You will learn about timeless blueprints for marriage, about commitment and communication, about romance and resolving conflict.

To make the most of your weekend, I encourage you to do four things:

*Dennis and
Barbara Rainey*

- Listen carefully during the messages and try to understand the overall purpose and plan for marriage, even if you're not sure you agree with a particular point at first. Many of the concepts and their application become more clear as the weekend progresses.

- Think about how you can apply the principles in your own life rather than focusing on what you think your spouse needs to learn.

- Commit to completing the couples' projects—they are crucial to the conference experience.

- Purpose to come up with at least two or three action points that you and your spouse agree to apply in the next 30 days by the end of the weekend.

As you return home on Sunday, we want you to leave with encouragement, hope, and practical tools to build your marriage and strengthen your legacy. And you'll understand why we call this conference a Weekend to Remember.

Yours for godly marriages and families,

Dennis Rainey

Dennis Rainey
Executive Director, FamilyLife

Conference Schedule

	TIME	TOPIC	PAGE	CONFEREE
F R I D A Y		Introduction/FamilyLife Information	1-32	
	7:00-7:40	**Welcome to your Weekend to Remember**		All
	7:40-7:50	Break (Resource Center open)		All
	7:50-8:40	**Five Threats to Oneness, Part I**	33	All
	8:40-8:55	Break (Resource Center open)		All
	8:55-10:00	**Five Threats to Oneness, Part II**		All
	10:00	Required Project (Complete before next session.)	42	All
		(Resource Center open)		
S A T U R D A Y	8:00-8:30	Resource Center open		
	8:30-9:30	**God's Purposes for Oneness**	45	All
	9:30-9:40	Break (Resource Center open)		All
	9:40-10:40	**God's Plan for Oneness**	53	All
	10:40-11:35	Required Project (Resource Center open)	61	Married
		Preparation for Marriage	67	Pre-married
	11:35-12:30	**God's Power for Oneness**	81	All
	12:30-2:00	Lunch (Resource Center open)		All
	2:00-3:30	**Understanding: Communication I**	91	All
	3:30-3:45	Break (Resource Center open)		All
	3:45-4:45	**Sexual Intimacy: Communication II**	111	All
		(Complete required project before Sunday sessions.)	120	
	4:45-5:45	**Engagement: Preparation for Marriage**	125	Pre-married
		(Resource Center open until 5:00 p.m.)		
	Sat. evening	Date Night		
S U N D A Y	*NOTE: Those staying in the hotel should check out after breakfast or during the lunch break.*			
	8:00-8:30	Resource Center open		
	8:30-9:30	**The Wife's Responsibility for Oneness**	131	All Women
		The Husband's Responsibility for Oneness	155	All Men
	9:30-9:40	Break (Resource Center open)		All
	9:40-10:30	**Mom**	143	All Women
		Dad	163	All Men
	10:30-11:25	Required Project (Resource Center open)	150,170	All
	11:25-12:30	**Resolving Conflict: Communication III**	175	All
	12:30-2:15	Lunch, Project, and Check Out (Resource Center open)	184	All
	1:45-2:15	Staff Opportunities Meeting (Room to be announced.)		Optional
	2:15-3:00	**Resolving Conflict Through the**	189	All
		Power of Blessing: Communication IV		
	3:00-3:15	Break (Resource Center open)		All
	3:15-4:15	**Leaving a Legacy of Destiny**	195	All
		Appendix (Resource Center open 15 minutes after last session)	201-256	

How can I make my marriage last?

How can I communicate with my spouse?

How can I raise my children?

How can I make the greatest contribution to my family and to future generations?

Effectively Developing Strong

One of the most urgent needs in our culture today is for answers to questions like these. One of our most heartfelt desires is to build a family where we can be loved and encouraged, and yet increasingly it seems that fewer and fewer people know how to reach that goal.

FAMILYLIFE™

Bringing Timeless Principles Home

That's why FamilyLife exists. We are a nonprofit organization designed to help people learn principles that will equip them to build the type of family they long for. We began in 1976 as a pre-marriage ministry for staff members of Campus Crusade for Christ. But the content proved so successful that people outside

FAMILIES

Campus Crusade began asking for it. Now FamilyLife has grown into a worldwide ministry with a variety of outreaches. The following pages describe a number of resources FamilyLife offers that are designed to help develop and strengthen your family.

CONFERENCES

Hundreds of thousands of couples have discovered an oasis in the midst of busy schedules by attending a Weekend to Remember™ conference. Not only do couples learn blueprints for marriage and family, but the conference also gives them the time to immediately apply what they learn.

Friday morning (before the conference), I had an appointment with a divorce attorney. Sunday afternoon, I recommitted my life to my marriage, my husband, and to God. I pray that my life will be forever changed.

Weekend to Remember attendee

Many couples leave the conference understanding for the first time how two selfish people can live together and love one another for a lifetime.

These weekend conferences also gave birth to Weekend to Remember Seminars held in churches across the country. And in 1999, we began a new type of conference designed to call couples to make a commitment to their marriage covenant. The I Still Do™ conferences and the new Rekindling the Romance™ conferences bring thousands of couples together in large arenas for a one-day celebration of marriage. More than one million people have attended FamilyLife Conferences.

Conference Information

For a list of upcoming conferences, call 1-800-FL-TODAY, 24 hours a day, or visit www.familylife.com on the Internet.

SMALL GROUPS

More than one million couples across America have experienced the life changing small group ministry of the HomeBuilders Couples Series® and the HomeBuilders Parenting Series®. These interactive studies are a powerful tool that not only helps couples continue to grow in their marriages, but also to teach others. "These studies have been used by laymen to help couples FamilyLife would never touch," says Dennis Rainey, FamilyLife president and creator of the series. "One of the most enjoyable comments I hear is someone leading a study and making a difference in the lives of their neighbors and community."

HomeBuilders Information

You'll find each of the different HomeBuilders studies at the Conference Resource Center—along with a HomeBuilders Starter pack to help you plan, promote, and lead a study. For more information on HomeBuilders, call 1-800-FL-TODAY, 24 hours a day, or visit www.familylife.com/homebuilders

CHURCH RESOURCES

FamilyLife helps pastors strengthen families through its seminars and through the Family Needs Survey. The easy-to-use survey could help your church build a family ministry that is focused, planned, and confident.

A Weekend to Remember seminar is an abridged version of the full Weekend to Remember conference. Churches across the country are hosting the day-and-a-half Weekend to Remember seminars or FamilyLife Parenting Seminars to strengthen marriages and families in their congregations and communities.

Church Resource Information

For information about our church seminars and Family Needs Survey, call 1-800-404-5052 (extension 2554), or visit www.familylife.com

RADIO

In 1992 we took the same vital message for families to the airwaves and launched "FamilyLife Today" on 17 radio stations. Today this award-winning broadcast—

supported almost entirely through donations from people like you—is heard Monday through Friday on hundreds of outlets (stations and translators) by an estimated audience of more than three million.

When you tune into FamilyLife's radio broadcasts, you discover ways to make your life and family work. Host Dennis Rainey, co-host Bob Lepine, and frequent guests produce messages on marriage and parenting that are timely, interesting, and practical. A wide variety of topics are addressed with honesty and wisdom.

Radio Information

To find out whether any of these shows are broadcast in your area, call 1-800-FL-TODAY or visit www.familylife.com on the Internet for stations and broadcast times.

I am a single mother of three children, and I am a full-time college student. I listen to your broadcast on the way to classes, and I am always touched by the messages you bring. Many times you have helped me to see the light at the end of the tunnel.

"FamilyLife Today" listener

The FamilyLife broadcast team
and their programs include (clockwise from far left):

Ashley Escue . . . ."FamilyLife This Week"

Bob Lepine . . . ."FamilyLife Today," "FamilyLife This Week"

Crawford Loritts . . . ."Living a Legacy"

Nancy Leigh DeMoss . . . ."Revive Our Hearts"

Dennis Rainey . . . ."FamilyLife Today"
"Real FamilyLife with Dennis Rainey"

Barbara Rainey . . . . Frequent guest on "FamilyLife Today"

INTERNATIONAL

Families around the world face daunting challenges. In many countries, individual rights are not upheld, women are degraded, and children are discarded. But "family" is an international language that crosses all borders, and FamilyLife has a growing international outreach.

From Spain to South Africa, from Germany to Greece, from Japan to Jamaica ... our borders continue to expand. Our goal is to assist, encourage, and train volunteers to reach out to families in their own countries. We have equipped individuals and organizations to reach families in approximately 100 countries. Hundreds of Weekend to Remember conferences have been held in nations around the world, and FamilyLife resources have been translated into more than two dozen languages or dialects.

We attended a Weekend to Remember conference in South Africa several years ago. We were so impressed that we organized additional FamilyLife Conferences and couples studies using the HomeBuilders Couples Series. We saw couples who were without hope become committed to each other. Now, after training in Little Rock, we have returned to begin a family-building organization in Pretoria. Our goal is to reach the entire continent of Africa.

—Quintus and Isolde Swanepoel
South Africa

FAMILY RESOURCES

Our resource emphasis began in 1985 with the publication of Dennis and Barbara Rainey's best-selling book, *Building Your Mate's Self-Esteem*. Since then we've continued building a growing line of products designed to equip you in building your marriage and family. These resources include:

In the past I would have never thought that such little things could add so much meaning and bring my husband and me closer together. Every couple should have Simply Romantic® Nights to let them know how wonderful the sexual relationship between a husband and wife is.

—Katy

- Books by Dennis and Barbara— including *Growing a Spiritually Strong Family*, *Two Hearts Praying as One*, and *Pressure Proof Your Marriage* from their new "Family First Series" and the re-release of *Staying Close*.

- "FamilyLife Today" audio series: We offer numerous packages of our most popular shows on marriage and parenting.

- True Connection™ products build your marriage or give you practical help in teaching biblical principles to your children. These popular packages include the best-selling Resurrection Eggs®, Simply Romantic® Nights, Simply Romantic® Secrets, Passport to Purity™, Adorenaments™, and Life Lessons™.

- "Best of the Best": The best books, tapes, and other resources we've found to equip you in marriage and parenting.

Family Resource Information

Be sure to visit the Conference Resource Center this weekend. You also can order resources by calling 1-800-FL-TODAY, 24 hours a day, or by visiting our online store at www.familylife.com

INTERNET

FamilyLife's Web site has become a trusted resource featuring a wealth of information designed to equip men and women to embrace god's truth for their marriages and families. With almost 6.5 million visits to www.familylife.com in 2003, people all over the world are looking for straight answers to the many challenges facing today's marriages and families.

The Family Room, FamilyLife's e-magazine, is an interactive experience for today's Christian family that includes:

- Articles by Christian leaders
- Audio links to FamilyLife Today broadcasts
- Printable resources
- Related links

Thanks for reminding me every day of what my job is as a Christian parent.

—Internet constituent

Please continue sending this incredible resource to us. I appreciate the articles and pictures.

—The Family Room subscriber

Visit

www.familylife.com

When the Honeymoon Ended

It didn't take long for Patrick and Leslie Cameron to realize that they were not as prepared for marriage as they thought. "Coming back from our honeymoon, we got into an argument," Patrick says. "Neither of us knew how to resolve conflict lovingly."

Both came from families in which there was divorce and separation, and each had an alcoholic parent. Patrick and Leslie were determined to be successful in their marriage, but their strong personalities and dogged determination led them into some relationship problems. "Our fights were ugly," Leslie says, "and I felt nobody else had problems like we had."

However, two months after their wedding, Patrick and Leslie attended a Weekend to Remember conference. "Realizing our spouse is not our enemy was a real eye-opener," Leslie says.

Patrick agrees, "We realized we had the same goals and desires but we were in disagreement on how to get there. With a new blueprint for marriage spelled out, we had the plan we needed to rebuild our relationship."

Now Patrick and Leslie attend a Weekend to Remember conference every year as an anniversary present to each other. Leslie says, "I hope other couples will understand what we finally realized—that just because you have conflict doesn't mean you're not supposed to be together."

OPPORTUNITIES
for Involvement

Why do men and women from all walks of life use the ministries and resources of FamilyLife? Because they are investing their lives in a cause greater than themselves.

Faithful ministry partners, loyal staff members, and dedicated volunteers are giving of their time, talent, and resources because of a passion for the family—a passion for bringing timeless principles home. These men and women are committed to changing the culture by changing families, one home at a time.

FamilyLife exists today because tens of thousands of ministry partners and volunteers across the nation share this passion. These dedicated men and women make financial donations, and help promote our conferences. They facilitate small-group studies using the HomeBuilders Couples Series®, or work in our international headquarters. The work of FamilyLife is their work, and it's possible only through their commitment.

> Ministry Partners
>
> Conference Promotion
>
> HomeBuilders Group Leader
>
> Ethnic Ministries
>
> Full-time Staff

Ministry Partners

As a non-profit organization, FamilyLife depends upon friends like you to help share timeless blueprints for the family around the world. Most of our operating budget comes from donations, and in addition, more than 120 husband and wife teams working at our headquarters are responsible for raising the funds necessary for their salary and benefits. No gift is insignificant, and no gift is too small or too large.

FamilyLife as an organization is a good investment. As a charter member of the Evangelical Council for Financial

Accountability (ECFA), we are not only audited annually, but we're also accountable for how we use your donations.

We are grateful for people like this mother who shared why she was committed to being a ministry partner:

> *I was writing out a check to FamilyLife when my daughter came to me and asked, "What is FamilyLife?" I told her it was an organization dedicated to keeping families together. She asked how much I was going to give. I was then completely shocked when she said, "Mommy, I want to give some of my own money if they will keep our family from divorcing."*

For more information on making a donation to FamilyLife, or on financially supporting a FamilyLife staff family, write to FamilyLife at 3900 North Rodney Parham Road, Little Rock, AR 72212-2441, or call 1-800-FL-TODAY, 24 hours a day. Our Internet address is www.familylife.com.

Conference Promotion

Many couples return home from a Weekend to Remember and begin thinking of all the people they know that could benefit from such an experience. If you're

interested in helping other couples have the same type of experience you've enjoyed at the conference, here are some opportunities to help promote future conferences in your area:

- City Team: Do you see yourself taking on a major role in expanding FamilyLife Conferences in your area? Consider being a part of the City Team. Help the local team by giving leadership to all the different aspects of promoting a conference, or even by leading a HomeBuilders strategy.

- Church Representative: Play a key role by keeping your church fully informed about upcoming conferences and other outreaches of FamilyLife.

- Conference Worker: Would you like to assist at next year's conference? Help with the tasks of greeting conferees, registering them quickly, and making resources available throughout the weekend at the Conference Resource Center.

■ Prayer Team: Play a crucial role in the spiritual battle being waged in homes by praying about the needs communicated to you by the City Team.

For more information, call 1-800-FL-TODAY, 24 hours a day, or contact www.familylife.com.

HomeBuilders Group Leader

In just a few weeks, continue to build a strong marriage, while also developing lifelong friendships, and helping other couples grow in their faith. Leading a small couples group using the HomeBuilders Couples Series® is not only fun, but it's also much easier than you think.

The leader's role is that of a facilitator—guiding the group through discussion questions and discovering together biblical principles for building a family. And each HomeBuilders study contains a leader's guide with helpful information and commentary to equip you in directing your group. In fact, we even offer a HomeBuilders Starter Pack that includes materials to promote and lead a group of four couples.

For more information about involvement in HomeBuilders, be sure to attend the HomeBuilders Orientation Special Session on Saturday afternoon. Also, visit the Conference Resource Center for copies of the HomeBuilders Starter Pack, and of the different HomeBuilders studies. After the conference, you can order HomeBuilders resources by calling 1-800-FL-TODAY, 24 hours a day, or by visiting www.familylife.com.

Ethnic Ministries

We work with a number of committed men and women to adapt our material for use in America's Asian, Spanish-speaking, and urban communities. For example, there are currently conferences and seminars in Spanish conducted around the country.

For more information on Spanish conferences, visit www.familylife.com, or call Hispanic FamilyLife at 1-877-FL-TODAY (1-877-358-6325), 24 hours a day. For information on outreaches in Asian communities, call Asian FamilyLife at 1-866-AFL-CCCI (1-866-235-2224).

Full-time Staff

Dentist. Banker. Engineer. Attorney. Editor. Chief Executive Officer. The FamilyLife staff team, headquartered in Little Rock, Ark., is composed of individuals from many walks of life. All are dedicated to helping you build your home so you can reach out to others with the same timeless principles for the family.

Almost 400 people now work in Little Rock, including more than 120 families

who raise their own financial support. **If you are interested in hearing more about full-time work with FamilyLife, or with our parent organization, Campus Crusade for Christ, be sure to attend the Staff Opportunities Meeting at 1:45 p.m. on the Sunday afternoon of the conference.**

Reaching Out in
an Upscale Neighborhood

The homes in their Baltimore neighborhood are upscale and well tended. But Jim and Barb Little had a hunch that looks were deceiving. Chances were that many of the marriages behind the doors of these affluent homes needed the same type of loving attention as the non-affluent did.

The Littles wanted to reach out to the couples in their neighborhood, but they lacked one thing. "We needed material to help us reach them," Barb says. When they attended a recent Weekend to Remember conference, they learned about the HomeBuilders Couples Series®. As Jim recalls, "We were convinced that HomeBuilders was the best way to expose our neighbors to the wisdom of God's plan for marriage without hitting them over the head with the Bible."

When they attended a training workshop after the conference, they left confident they could lead a group. "We felt anyone can do this!" Barb recalls.

After deciding to co-lead the group with some friends, Jim and Barb invited 17 couples to a barbecue where they would hear about the HomeBuilders study. Eventually, seven couples signed up and attended faithfully more than two years, working through two studies. Says Barb, "All of the marriages improved spiritually, including ours," Barb says.

Through HomeBuilders, the Littles saw that God's Word crosses all boundaries. Jim states we often assume successful people cannot be reached with the gospel because of their prosperity. But he believes their group proves otherwise. "Most successful people know how to recognize a good deal," he says. "And God's plan for marriage is a good deal!"

One HOME at a Time

As a country, we are healthier, but not happier. We are drenched in knowledge, but parched for wisdom. The most prosperous nation the world has ever known suffers from a sickness in its soul.

Nowhere is this more apparent than in the state of the family. The values that built our great nation—once passed on from each generation to the next as a national treasure—are now dismissed. As a result, our homes are deteriorating at an alarming rate.

Psalm 127:1 states, "Unless the Lord builds the house, they labor in vain who build it." We believe that homes will be transformed as people turn to God and His Word for direction in their lives. And as homes are transformed, our culture is transformed—one home at a time.

My hope is that your experience at this Weekend to Remember Conference will light a spiritual fire within your soul that will never be extinguished. Allow God to transform you and your family, and then ask Him for opportunities to reach out to others with the love of Christ.

I also hope you've caught a glimpse of how FamilyLife can help you and your family. As we look at our culture and at a long history of God's faithfulness, we see the need to continue expanding our ministry in the United States and around the world through conferences, radio, small groups, resources, the Internet, and much more. We never lose our focus of ministering to families like yours. When you need resources and training for your marriage and family, think of FamilyLife.

Dennis Rainey

Dennis Rainey
Executive Director, FamilyLife

FamilyLife Conference Speakers

A voice of experience. A voice of understanding.

Our speakers have come to understand thoroughly the importance of God's blueprints for marriage and are living it out in their daily lives. They are a dynamic, fun-filled group of people who are committed to both encourage and equip you and your spouse to build a godly home. Their presentations are biblically and professionally sound. It is FamilyLife's hope that you will enjoy and gain great insight from their unique perspectives on how putting God's plan into action will change your marriage for the better ... forever.

Barry and Pam Abell

Barry and Pam serve as director and co-director respectively of Executive Ministries, an affiliated ministry of Campus Crusade for Christ. Barry received his bachelor of arts degree in business from Austin Peay State University and worked as a municipal bond trader for 21 years on Wall Street. Pam received her master of science in elementary education from Montclair State University. The Abells have two children and four grandchildren, and reside in Lakewood, Pa.

Dan and Becky Allender

Dan and Becky live in Bainbridge Island, Wash., where Dan serves as president of Mars Hill Graduate School. He is the author of several books including *The Wounded Heart* and *The Healing Path*. Becky is a homemaker and landscape architect with a master of arts degree in education from Colorado Christian University. The Allenders have three children.

Jose and Michelle Alvarez

Jose played professional baseball for 16 years and now serves as a chaplain for the Atlanta Braves AA team in Greenville, S.C. In addition to ministering to professional baseball couples, Jose and Michelle also teach marriage and parenting classes at their church. Jose is vice president of marketing for SportWorx, a sports risk insurance agency. Michelle studied nursing and now serves as a fulltime homemaker. The Alverezes have three children.

Jim and Anne Arkins

Jim is a graduate of the University of Arkansas College of Medicine and works as a family practice physician in Bentonville, Ark. Anne completed her degree in secondary education from the University of Arkansas. She has authored *Watchmen on the Walls*, a book about praying for your children, and other women's Bible study materials. Jim and Anne are the parents of four children and the grandparents of eight.

Bruce and Julie Boyd

Bruce and Julie have served together for 20 years in the concert outreach of Campus Crusade for Christ's Keynote ministry. Keynote addresses family and marriage issues through both musical and other artistic expression. Bruce graduated from the University of Illinois with a degree in music education; Julie received a bachelor's degree in business management from Texas Wesleyan University, and homeschools their three boys. The Boyds live in Fishers, Ind.

Charles and Karen Boyd

Charles serves as teaching pastor of Southside Fellowship in Greenville, S.C., and received his doctorate of ministry from Gordon-Conwell Theological Seminary. He has authored *Different Children, Different Needs* along with *The Understanding One Another Profile*. Karen received her bachelor of science in secondary education from Florida State University and enjoys homemaking. The Boyds have three children and live in Simpsonville, S.C.

Dan and Julie Brenton

Dan serves as senior pastor of Fellowship Bible Church in Roswell, Ga. As a staff member with Campus Crusade for Christ for 17 years he worked as director of the Communication Center. Julie is a graduate of Kansas University where she received a degree in elementary education. Julie and Dan are the parents of three children and live in Marietta, Ga.

Raymond and Donna Causey

Raymond, former director of Urban Family Ministries, now pastors a church in Atlanta. He received his bachelor of arts in communications and biblical studies from Biola University, and is the author of *Changing for Good*. His wife Donna is a homemaker, Bible teacher, and mentor. The Causeys live in Riverdale, Ga., with their four children.

Karl and Junanne Clauson

Karl is a teaching pastor at ChangePoint in Anchorage, Alaska. He and his wife Junanne are graduates of Multnomah Bible College where they received bachelor of science degrees in biblical studies. Junanne is a homemaker, mentor, and ministry partner. The Clausons have two children.

Doug and Patty Daily

Doug is the teaching pastor at Woodland Park Community Church near Colorado Springs, Colo. He is a graduate of Mississippi State University and Dallas Theological Seminary and has received his doctorate of ministry from Bethel Seminary. Doug is the author of *Overcoming Stress in Your Marriage*. Patty graduated from the University of Wisconsin-LaCrosse and teaches reading to children with learning disabilities. The Dailys have three children.

Kyle and Sharon Dodd

Kyle is the executive director of Camp Timberline in Estes Park, Colo., a Christian sports and mountain adventure camp for youth. He is also a teaching pastor at Cherry Hills Community Church. Sharon has a degree in physical and special education, and she and Kyle have written teen devotionals and a devotional book, *Family Matters*. Kyle has also authored *A Cut Above* and *Avoiding Parental Landmines*. The Dodds live in Castle Rock, Colo., with their four sons.

Tim and Joy Downs

Tim and Joy serve as Campus Crusade for Christ staff members in Cary, N.C. Tim is the author of *Finding Common Ground*, for which he received the Gold Medallion Book Award in recognition of excellence in evangelical Christian literature. Both Tim and Joy are graduates of Indiana State University, where he received a bachelor of arts in fine arts and she received her bachelor of science degree in journalism. The Downses have three children.

Michael and Cindy Easley

Michael is senior pastor/teacher of Immanuel Bible Church in Springfield, Va. After he and Cindy completed bachelor's degrees at Stephen F. Austin State University, Michael earned a master of theology degree from Dallas Theological Seminary, where he is now working on his doctorate. Cindy is a homemaker, Bible teacher, and retreat speaker. The Easleys have four children.

Dennis and Jill Eenigenburg

Dennis is teaching pastor of The Chapel on the Campus at Louisiana State University in Baton Rouge, La. Following graduation from Calvary Bible College, he received both his master's and doctorate of ministry degrees from Dallas Theological Seminary. Dennis is the author of *Workbook on Morality*, and he and Jill co-authored *Expressing Love in Your Marriage*. Jill studied music at Moody Bible Institute and teaches piano. The Eenigenburgs have three sons and four grandchildren.

Joe and Cindi Ferrini

Joe has practiced dentistry for 24 years and serves on the National Board of Directors for the Medical Ministry of Campus Crusade for Christ. He and Cindi serve as associate staff members with Campus Crusade and they direct discipleship ministry in their local church. Cindi is a homemaker and seminar speaker. She has also authored a Bible study entitled *Balancing the Active Life* and an organizational workbook *Get It Together*. The Ferrinis live in Cleveland, Ohio, with their three children.

Tom and Toni Fortson

Tom is president and chief executive officer of Promise Keepers® Men of Integrity, and serves on the board of directors for the Moody Bible Institute. A graduate of Iowa State University, Tom received master's and doctorate degrees from Michigan State University. Toni received her bachelor of arts in business education from the University of Michigan and is a homemaker and women's Bible study leader. The Fortsons have three children and live in Centennial, Colo.

Jerry and Nancy Foster

Jerry is a certified financial planner and chief executive officer of Foster Group, a financial planning and life coaching company in West Des Moines, Iowa. He also serves as a speaker for CrossTrainers, a weekly men's group of 600. Nancy is a registered nurse but serves as fulltime wife and mother. She also leads women's Bible studies and mentoring groups. Jerry and Nancy lead a local Fellowship of Christian Athlete's group and have been involved in foster care for numerous children. The Fosters reside in Adel, Iowa, and have four children.

James and Cynthia Gorton

James and Cynthia are professional certified counselors and corporate business consultants. They served previously with Campus Crusade for Christ, as well as in pastoral ministry. James received a doctorate in psychology from The Union Institute. Cynthia earned her master's in counseling and her doctorate in educational leadership and policy studies from Arizona State University. They have co-authored a book entitled *Priceless Investments*. The Gortons live in Scottsdale, Ariz., with their three children.

Floyd and Diana Green

Floyd is a certified financial planner and president of Cornerstone Financial Consultants in Raleigh, N.C. He graduated from North Carolina State University and holds master's degrees from Wheaton Graduate School and Dallas Theological Seminary. Diana is also a graduate of North Carolina State and is now a homemaker and ministers to women in the area of parenting issues. The Greens live in Raleigh, N.C., with their six children.

Doug and Susan Grimes

Doug is pastor of Oak Grove Covenant Church in Lexington, Ky., and received his master of divinity from Asbury Theological Seminary. Susan received a bachelor of arts in interior design/housing from the University of Kentucky. Susan and Doug spent 11 years ministering with Campus Crusade for Christ in Utah and Kentucky. They have three children.

Dick and Nancy Hastings

Dick served as a pastor for 10 years, and is now a Life Skills educator and marriage coach. He and his wife, Nancy, were associated for more than six years with Campus Crusade for Christ; three with the European music group MasterPeace. Dick is a Vietnam veteran (U.S.M.C.) and received his master of divinity degree from Western Conservative Baptist Seminary. Nancy is a graduate of West Virginia University and is admissions director at a local Christian school. The Hastingses have four children and live near Tuscaloosa, Ala.

Bruce and Janet Hess

Bruce is a teaching pastor at Wildwood Community Church in Norman, Okla., with extensive ministry experience in the country of Latvia, including a weekly radio broadcast. He earned a degree in broadcast journalism from the University of Nebraska and a master of theology from Dallas Theological Seminary. Janet is also a graduate of the University of Nebraska and is a former public school teacher. She is a wife and mother, and works part-time outside the home. The Hesses have four children.

Alan and Theda Hlavka

Alan serves as teaching pastor at Good Shepherd Community Church near Portland, Ore. He has a master of arts degree in theology from Western Seminary and a bachelor's degree from Lewis and Clark College. Theda is a homemaker and author of the book *Saying "I Do" Was the Easy Part*. Alan and Theda have three children and two grandchildren and live in Gresham, Ore.

Bob and Jan Horner

Bob and Jan have served as staff members with Campus Crusade for Christ since 1964. Bob has authored several Bible study guides, and he and Jan co-authored *Resolving Conflict in Your Marriage*. He holds a mechanical engineering degree from the University of Colorado. Jan studied business at Colorado State University and helped establish M.O.P.S. International, an organization serving mothers of preschoolers. Bob and Jan have three children and four grandchildren and live in Boulder, Colo.

Joel and Cindy Housholder

Joel and Cindy work with Search Ministries in the Dallas area. Before joining Search, the Housholders ministered with Young Life for 20 years, and Joel served as regional director of Young Life in northeast Texas for 10 years. Joel received his master of theology degree from Dallas Theological Seminary and is pursuing his doctorate from Fuller Seminary. Cindy is a graduate of Southern Methodist University where she received her bachelor of arts degree in fine arts. The Housholders have three children.

Bill and Terri Howard

Bill serves as area director of Search Ministries with his wife, Terri, in Nashville. He also served with Campus Crusade for Christ for 11 years—10 with FamilyLife, where he authored the Family Manifesto. He is a graduate of Idaho State University and Dallas Theological Seminary. Terri is a graduate of Auburn University with a degree in public relations. The Howards have four sons.

Dan and Kathie Jarrell

Dan is a teaching pastor at ChangePoint in Anchorage, Alaska. He also served as teaching pastor at Fellowship Bible Church in Little Rock, Ark., and helped establish Fellowship Bible Church in Conway, Ark. Dan completed his undergraduate degree in geology at Southern Oregon State University, and has a master's degree in theology from Western Conservative Baptist Seminary. Kathie graduated from Multnomah School of the Bible and is a homemaker. The Jarrells have five children.

Ron and Mary Jenson

Ron is the chairman of Future Achievement International, a personal leadership training and coaching company. He is also an international speaker and the author of several books, including *Achieving Authentic Success*. A past president of the International School of Theology, Ron has served as chairman of High Ground Associates (a worldwide association of business executives). Mary is a homemaker and the author of several resources including Partners in Promise. She serves on the board of Moms in Touch, Int'l. The Jensons live in San Diego, and are the parents of two children.

Dave and Peggy Jones

Dave is senior pastor of Gwinnett Community Church near Atlanta. A graduate of Wheaton College, Dave also served as pastor of FamilyLife Ministries for a large church in northern California. He and Peggy worked with Campus Crusade for Christ for nine years. Peggy, an interior decorator, has often teamed with Dave in counseling and teaching on home and family issues. The Joneses have three children and four grandchildren.

Jim and Renee Keller

Jim is the founder and president of Charis Counseling Center in Orlando, Fla., where he specializes in marriage and family counseling. He and his wife, Renee, have more than 50 years of combined ministry experience on the staff of Campus Crusade for Christ. Jim graduated from the University of Toledo and has a master's degree in marriage and family therapy from Springfield College. Renee graduated from the University of South Florida, and works with Campus Crusade in the president's office. The Kellers have two children.

Tim and Darcy Kimmel

Tim and Darcy have been speaking on family issues for more than two decades. Tim is the executive director of Family Matters and is a well-known radio host. The author of several books, he wrote *Little House on the Freeway* and *Basic Training for a Few Good Men*. Darcy is a homemaker, speaker, and co-author of *The Home Maintenance Manual: 301 Ways to Give Rest to Your Hurried Home*. The Kimmels have four children and live in Scottsdale, Ariz.

Bob and Mary Ann Lepine

Bob is director and co-host of "FamilyLife Today," FamilyLife's nationally syndicated and award-winning radio broadcast. Author of *The Christian Husband*, Bob also serves on the board of directors for the National Religious Broadcasters (NRB). Mary Ann is a homemaker, who also holds a bachelor of science degree in nursing. The Lepines live in Little Rock, Ark., and have five children.

Crawford and Karen Loritts

Crawford is associate director of U.S. Ministries with Campus Crusade for Christ, and the author of several resources including *Never Walk Away* and *Lessons From a Life Coach*. He also hosts the nationally broadcast "Living a Legacy" radio program. Karen is a conference and retreat speaker, and has authored articles for publication including *A Mother's Legacy*. The Lorittses have four children and one grandchild, and live in Fairburn, Ga.

Bob and Judi Maddox

Bob is the pastor of leadership development at Good Shepherd Community Church near Portland, Ore., where he served as pastor of adult discipleship for 12 years. Judi is a homemaker and has been actively involved with Moms in Touch. Bob and Judi graduated from Fresno State University and served as staff members with Campus Crusade for Christ for 13 years. Bob received a master's degree in pastoral ministries from Western Conservative Baptist Seminary. Married for 28 years, the Maddoxes have five children and live in Gresham, Ore.

Doug and Amy Martin

Doug serves as vice president of Internet Services and Hope for Orphans for FamilyLife in Little Rock, Ark. He received his bachelor of science degree in business administration from Bowling Green State University in Ohio. Amy obtained her bachelor of science in nursing from Ohio State University. She is a homemaker. The Martins are the parents of six children and live in Roland, Ark.

Bob and Liz McEwen

Bob speaks internationally on pro-family and free market issues, and is president of Freedom Quest, a business development and investment firm. He served 20 years in elective office, including six years in the Ohio legislature and 12 years in the United States Congress, representing Ohio. Liz was an international flight attendant for six years and is now an image consultant and seminar leader with The Crowning Touch. The McEwens have four children, and live in Fairfax Station, Va.

Ray and Robyn McKelvy

Ray is a co-pastor and co-founder of New Hope Bible Church in Kansas City, Mo. He also serves on the board of directors of Calvary Bible College and Theological Seminary in Kansas City, Mo. Robyn is a fulltime homemaker who homeschools the couple's seven children.

David and Shari Meserve

David serves as teaching pastor of Cherry Hills Community Church in Highlands Ranch, Colo. He received his master of divinity degree from Denver Seminary and a master in counseling from Colorado Christian University. Shari received a master's degree in counseling from Colorado Christian and is a homemaker. The couple lives in Littleton, Colo., and has three children.

Tim and Noreen Muehlhoff

Tim is the director of applied communication at the Communication Center in Cary, N.C. He is also completing his doctorate in communication theory from the University of North Carolina at Chapel Hill. The Muehlhoffs were instrumental in initiating campus ministry in the nation of Lithuania. Noreen graduated from the University of Connecticut with a degree in business and has served with Campus Crusade for Christ since 1984. She is a fulltime homemaker. The couple has three children.

Bill and Pam Mutz

Bill is the president of Lakeland Ford in Lakeland, Fla., and has been involved with the ministries of FamilyLife, Promise Keepers, and his local church for many years. Pam graduated as a physical education major from the University of Northern Colorado and coaches children's team sports. She also leads women's Bible studies. Bill and Pam are the parents of 12 children.

Johnny and Leslyn Parker

Johnny oversees spiritual encouragement at First Baptist Church of Glenarden in Landover, Md. He also serves as director for the Relationship Fitness Group, where he conducts seminars for building strong relationships. Johnny has authored *Blueprints for Marriage: Building Love for a Lifetime* and received a master of arts degree in counseling psychology from Bowie State University in Maryland. Leslyn is a graduate of Liberty University and is a homemaker and Mary Kay consultant. The Parkers live in Beltsville, Md., with their three children.

Dick and Paula Purnell

Dick is the executive director of Single Life Resources, a ministry of Campus Crusade for Christ. He has authored 12 books, including the best sellers *Becoming a Friend and Lover* and *Growing Closer to God*. Dick holds a master's degree in education—specializing in counseling—from Indiana University, and a master of divinity degree from Trinity International University. Paula graduated from East Carolina University and often speaks with Dick at conferences and seminars. They live in Raleigh, N.C., with their two children.

Dennis and Barbara Rainey

Dennis serves as president of FamilyLife in Little Rock, Ark., where he and Barbara helped found the ministry in 1976. The Raineys have written numerous books together, including *Moments Together for Couples* and *Parenting Today's Adolescent*. Dennis also hosts the nationally syndicated "FamilyLife Today" broadcast. The Raineys graduated from the University of Arkansas, and Dennis later earned a master's degree in biblical studies from Dallas Theological Seminary. They have six children and five grandchildren.

Brett and Carol Ray

Brett and Carol are the founders of Right Choice Communications, a nonprofit organization that ministers to teenagers around the globe. The Rays have also ministered to pastors and their wives in St. Petersburg, Russia. Brett is an ordained minister and serves on the teaching team at his home church in Michigan. After a 10-year career as a registered nurse, Carol now works at home as a fulltime wife and mom. The Rays live in Holly, Mich., with their five children.

Gary and Barbara Rosberg

Gary and Barbara Rosberg are authors and speakers on marriage- and family-related issues. Gary founded CrossTrainers, a men's ministry that meets on a weekly basis. Their nationally syndicated radio program "The Rosbergs, America's Family Coaches … Live!" is heard daily. Gary has authored *Dr. Rosberg's Do-it-Yourself Relationship Mender* and co-authored *The Five Love Needs of Men and Women* with Barbara. The Rosbergs are currently launching a new campaign, Divorce Proofing America's Marriages. They have two children and one grandchild, and live outside Des Moines.

Mark and Lisa Schatzman

Mark is a teaching pastor at Grace Church in Little Rock, Ark. Previously, he served for seven years with FamilyLife as director of marketing and strategic planning, marketing manager, and director of conference ministry. He graduated from the University of New Mexico with a degree in communication and writing. Lisa is also a graduate of the University of New Mexico and is a homemaker and part-time teacher. The Schatzmans live in Little Rock, Ark., with their four children.

Jeff and Brenda Schulte

Jeff is a cofounder and teaching pastor of Fellowship Bible Church in Franklin, Tenn. A graduate of Yale University and Western Seminary, he co-authored the best selling pre-marriage guide *Preparing for Marriage*, and co-edited *The Big Picture: The Bible in Seven Minutes a Day*. Brenda earned a bachelor's degree from Moorhead State University and is a featured vocalist on "Experiencing God: Music for Knowing and Doing the Will of God." She is a fulltime wife and mother. The Schultes have six children and reside in Brentwood, Tenn.

Clarence and Brenda Shuler

Clarence is co-pastor of Northview Evangelical Free Church and president of Building Lasting Relationships. He also serves on the board of Koinonia House, a ministry to former prison inmates. Clarence has authored *Winning the Race to Unity: Is Reconciliation Really Working?* and *Your Wife Can Be Your Best Friend*. Brenda received her master's degree in religious education and is a homemaker. The Shulers have three children and live in Colorado Springs, Colo.

Chuck and Beth Simmons

Chuck serves as judge of South Carolina's Circuit Court. In addition to degrees in political science and criminal justice from East Tennessee State University, he completed his juris doctorate at the University of South Carolina. Beth received her bachelor of science degree in education from the University of Georgia and was an elementary school teacher prior to becoming a fulltime homemaker. The Simmonses live in Greenville, S.C., with their three children.

Greg and Bonnie Speck

Greg is a youth specialist for Reign Ministries and the author of *Sex, It's Worth Waiting For* and *Living for Jesus When the Party's Over*. He is a graduate of Bethel College. Bonnie is a public school nurse and the mother of their four children. The Specks live in Rockford, Ill.

Gary and Luci Stanley

Gary and Luci work with Global Community Resources, a ministry of Campus Crusade for Christ. The Stanleys served at the International School of Theology for 20 years—Gary as a communication professor and Luci as the associate director of field ministry. He is the author of several books, including *What My Dog Taught Me About Life* and *How to Make a Moose Run*. The Stanleys make their home near Boulder, Colo.

David and Sande Sunde

Dave and Sande serve internationally with Global Community Resources. Cofounders of FamilyLife, they have authored several books including Dave's *Growing Together in Christ* and resources for Christians in the marketplace. Both are graduates of Western Michigan University. The parents of three children and the grandparents of 13 grandchildren, Dave and Sande live in Louisville, Colo.

Rick and Judy Taylor

Rick is a pastor at Fellowship Bible Church in Little Rock, Ark., and the author of *When Life Is Changed Forever*. He graduated from the University of Texas, Arlington, received his masters and doctorate degrees from Dallas Theological Seminary, and completed two years of postgraduate study at Emporia State University. Judy attended Biola University, and is a homemaker, mentor, and longtime children's Bible story teacher. The Taylors have three children and two grandchildren.

Roger and Joanne Thompson

Roger is senior pastor of Berean Baptist Church in Burnsville, Minn. He received a degree in human relations from Westmont College in Santa Barbara, Calif., and a master of divinity degree from Denver Seminary. Joanne is also a graduate of Westmont College, and is a homemaker and an active leader of women's Bible studies. The Thompsons live in Apple Valley, Minn., and have two children and one grandchild.

J.T. and Enid Walker

J. T. is pastor of community outreach at Immanuel Bible Church in Springfield, Va. The Walkers served for more than 20 years with Campus Crusade for Christ and coordinated campus ministry for several historically black colleges. J.T. and Enid received degrees in clinical psychology—J. T. from Morehouse College, and Enid from Spelman College. Enid is a homemaker and the mother of their five children.

Chris and Susan Willard

Chris and Susan serve on the staff of Campus Crusade for Christ in Orlando, Fla., and Chris is director of the Innovation Center for Technology. He received his bachelor of arts degree in history and political science from the University of Massachusetts, and his master of business administration from Belhaven College. Susan, also a graduate of the University of Massachusetts, received her bachelor of fine arts degree in painting and graphic design. She is a homemaker and women's ministry leader. The Willards have three children.

John and Linda Willett

John is the area and division director for Search Ministries in Greensboro, N.C. John and Linda both graduated from Allegheny College with bachelor of arts degrees in sociology. John also received his master of divinity degree from Grace Seminary. Linda assists her husband in his work, is active in women's ministries, and serves as a homemaker. The Willetts have two children and three grandchildren.

Dave and Ann Wilson

Dave received a master of divinity degree from the International School of Theology, and serves as teaching pastor at the Kensington Community Church in Troy, Mich. Inducted into the Men's Athletic Hall of Fame at Ball State University, Dave is also chaplain to the Detroit Lions. Ann attended the University of Kentucky, and ministers to wives of professional athletes. She is a homemaker. The Wilsons have three children and live in Rochester Hills, Mich.

Jerry and Sheryl Wunder

Jerry and Sheryl live in East Asia where Jerry is vice president of operations with a training and consulting company, and Sheryl assists in leadership development and mentoring. Prior to serving for 13 years with FamilyLife in various leadership positions, Jerry was also a business executive. He and Sheryl graduated from the University of South Carolina, and they have co-authored *Expressing Love in Your Marriage*. The Wunders have three children.

John and Susan Yates

For the past 20 years, John has been the rector of the historic Falls Church in Falls Church, Va., and has authored several resources, including *How a Man Prays for His Family*. Susan is a freelance speaker and author of several books, including *And Then I Had Teenagers: Encouragement for Parents of Teens and Pre-Teens*. She is also a columnist for Today's Christian Woman magazine. John and Susan are the parents of five children.

Five Threats to Oneness

Five Threats to Oneness

 ## Sessions 1 and 2 Overview

*Identifying forces that attempt to destroy
a marriage help a husband and wife move toward oneness.*

Introduction

- Maintaining oneness is the critical issue in marriage.

- How does an enthusiastic, optimistic, and hopeful marriage turn into a disaster?

- Couples today are threatened by forces that can destroy oneness in marriage.

I. Threat No. 1: Difficult adjustments threaten our oneness.

A. There is little in our ___culture___ today that encourages two people to make the difficult adjustments required to achieve marital oneness.

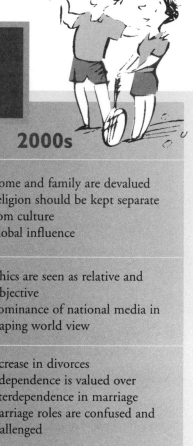

Sociological Change and the Family

1900s	AREA OF CHANGE	2000s
• Home and family were highly valued • Religion was an esteemed part of culture • Local/national influence	Society	• Home and family are devalued • Religion should be kept separate from culture • Global influence
• Judeo-Christian ethic • Emergence of national media (television, radio, Internet) as the primary influence of world view	World View	• Ethics are seen as relative and subjective • Dominance of national media in shaping world view
• Commitment is valued • Marriage is seen as an interdependent relationship • Marriage roles were commonly accepted	Marriage	• Increase in divorces • Independence is valued over interdependence in marriage • Marriage roles are confused and challenged
• Present and active	Fathers	• Passive and/or absent
• Valued and esteemed	Mothers	• Devalued and disparaged
• Blessing	Children	• Burden
• Family life was imperfect but intact	Result	• Family life is fragmented and facing difficult challenges

Your marriage is being influenced by rapid changes in our culture.

B. Contrasting _____backgrounds_____ bring about painful adjustments for a couple in the following areas:

- Values

- Vocations

- Religion

- Finances

- Family history

- Past relationships

- Painful experiences

C. The following superficial _____motivations_____ for marriage require shocking adjustments:

- Feelings

- Sexual attraction/involvement

- Cultural or family pressures

- Escape

D. Differing _____expectations_____ about marriage in the following areas result in unexpected adjustments:

- Roles

- Expression of love

- Sexual performance

- Plans for the future

Threat No. 1
RESULT

When couples fail to make necessary adjustments to move toward oneness, isolation is inevitable.

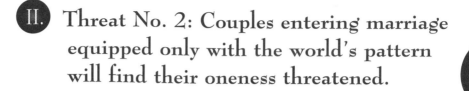
II. Threat No. 2: Couples entering marriage equipped only with the world's pattern will find their oneness threatened.

A. The world's pattern is a 50/50 _performance_ relationship.

    1. Acceptance is based upon performance—"You do your part, and I'll do mine."

    2. Giving is based upon merit—affection is given when one feels it is deserved.

    3. Motivation for action is based upon how one feels.

B. The world's pattern (50/50 performance relationship) is destined to

    self destruct because of:

    1. My inability to meet unreal expectations

    2. The impossibility of knowing my spouse has met me halfway

    3. My tendency to focus on weaknesses in my spouse

    4. My disappointment in my spouse, which paralyzes my performance

    5. My desire to get revenge when wronged

       disappointment
       hurt
       coldness
       revenge

Threat No. 2 **RESULT**	*The logical result of the world's pattern for marriage is isolation.*

III. Threat No. 3: The failure to anticipate selfishness in marriage threatens oneness.

I&2

A. Everyone has a natural tendency to be _selfish/self centered_ and destructive in relationships.

 All of us like sheep have gone astray, each of us has turned to his own way ... Isaiah 53:6a

I, If feel, want... blame game I'm victim what I deserve

B. Our culture today promotes and encourages _individualism_.

C. Because we marry with "stars in our eyes," we cannot see this _reality_.

1. During dating there is usually little daily responsibility and pressure.

2. Early in the relationship appreciation and approval are freely reflected.

D. This selfishness will rob the relationship of its _romance_.

ability to focus on well being of other person.

1. Our selfish nature focuses on and becomes critical of our spouse's weaknesses or failure to meet <u>our</u> expectations.

2. Our disappointment and disapproval of our spouse leads to feelings of rejection, discouragement, anger, and bitterness, resulting in even lower performance.

3. Our selfish nature even seeks to justify our rejection of our spouse.

Threat No. 3 **RESULT**	*The devastating result of selfishness is isolation.*

Life is not about making us happy

IV. Threat No. 4: A failure to work through ~~inevitable~~ *guaranteed* difficulties and trials threatens oneness.

1&2

A. There are two failures in our response to trials.

   1. There is a failure to ___anticipate___ the certainty of difficulties and problems.

   2. There is a failure to ___respond___ ___properly___ to difficulties and problems.

B. Difficulties do not mean something is wrong with your marriage.

C. God will allow difficulties in your life for many reasons. (James 1:2-6) ↓

NEED trials to grow strong

D. Your ___response___ to difficulties will either drive you apart or bind you together.

   1. Some respond to problems by trying to suppress or escape the pressure.

   2. Others respond to problems by blaming or attacking others.

   3. You must have a plan to move through these periods without rejecting or withdrawing from your spouse.

when pain lean into it

Threat No. 4 **RESULT**	*A failure to grasp God's perspective together on these problems will result in isolation.*

FIVE THREATS TO ONENESS

V. Threat No. 5: Extramarital "affairs" threaten oneness.

A. An extramarital "affair" is an ___ESCape___ from reality or

a ___search___ for fulfillment outside the marriage.

attempt to meet legit needs w/ illegit means

B. Extramarital "affairs" take many different forms:

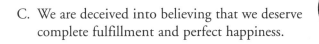

• Activities affair *(stay busy)*

buy things you don't need w/ $ you don't have

• Materialism affair

• Career affair

• Family affair

• Love affair

C. We are deceived into believing that we deserve complete fulfillment and perfect happiness.

1. Society programs people.

2. People develop an improper perception of reality.

3. People compare their expectations and fantasies to real life.

4. People begin to question reality (and not their fantasies).

5. People escape to extramarital affairs.

6. People ultimately end up in isolation.

Threat No. 5 RESULT	*The escape to extramarital affairs dooms a relationship to isolation.*

1 & 2

Romantic Phase

(dating, honeymoon)

- Oneness and happiness are goals, but the couple has no plan to achieve them.
- The social, physical, and emotional relationship is an incomplete picture of marriage.
- Intense feelings characterize this phase, but they cannot be sustained.

Transition Phase

(honeymoon or early marriage)

- A couple begins to make adjustments to each other in their values, habits, and expectations.
- Twinges of disappointment strike the heart, but they are either quickly extinguished by overwhelming feelings for each other, or they are ignored.

Reality Phase

- The relationship begins to take on a new dimension as the following press in: Moving to an unfamiliar environment, differing friends, job changes and stress, conflicting material values, children and parenting pressures, parental and in-law expectations and interference, difficulties and problems of life, conflicting financial philosophies.
- The realities of life sober the relationship, and feelings begin to vary greatly.
- The struggle to change each other sets in.

Retaliation Phase

- Emotional or even physical retaliation becomes an alternative.
- Resentment and bitterness begin to take their toll.
- A man sells his life out to his profession or interests outside the home.
- A woman pours her life into her children, seeks social identity outside the home, or seeks a new career.
- Marriage is no longer viewed with expectancy, but with despair.

Rejection Phase

- Physical separation— DIVORCE. The heart is so hardened that even the known consequences and the unknown future are overridden by hostility or discouragement.
- Emotional separation— WITHDRAWAL. Emotional withdrawal takes place and the relationship dies.

I just called to say I love you   *She'll △ give her time*   *You've lost that lovin' feeling*   *unplugged heart*

Unless the LORD builds the house, they labor in vain who build it.
Psalm 127:1a

God's Purposes for Marriage

God's Plan for Marriage

God's Power for Marriage

God's Process for Marriage

God's Product for Marriage: Oneness

Five Threats to Oneness

Application Project

This application project has two sections: the individual section and the interaction section. Be sure to leave adequate time to interact as a couple on the interaction section.

Individual Section

10 Minutes

Setting: Stay together as a couple, but complete this section quickly without any interaction.

Objective: To gain insight into how much the Five Threats have affected your marriage.

Instructions: Rate how much each threat has affected your marriage by checking the appropriate box. (Refer to your notes if necessary.) Explain what results have occurred in your marriage because of each threat.

THREATS	HOW MUCH EFFECT			RESULTS IN MY MARRIAGE CAUSED BY THIS THREAT
	LITTLE	SOME	SIGNIFICANT	
1. Difficult adjustments	☐	☐	☑	hurt bitterness
2. World's 50/50 pattern	☐	☐	☑	disappointment hurt coldness
3. Selfishness	☐	☐	☑	romance is gone
4. Difficulties, trials, and problems	☑	☐	☐	
5. Extramarital "affairs"	☑	☐	☐	

Interaction Section

20-30 Minutes

Setting: Stay together for interaction. Find a place where you are able to talk freely.

Objective: To share and gain insight on how your marriage has been affected by these threats.

Instructions:

1. Review how the Five Threats to Oneness have affected your relationship. Be considerate and teachable.

2. Agree on one or two specific action points to protect yourselves against those threats that are most dangerous to your marriage.

3. Write one point of action you will take individually or as a couple on the Take It Home page.

4. Record that point of action on the Take It Home Summary flap attached to the back cover.

Take It Home

INDIVIDUAL APPLICATION

I will do this! Check one or more of the following:

☐ Because the 50-50 pattern has threatened our marriage, I will compliment my spouse about something at least once a day for the next two weeks.

☐ Since I am likely blinded to my own subtle selfishness, I will ask my spouse to carefully identify (with sensitivity) an area where to him I appear selfish. Then I will make needed adjustments.

☐ Realizing how much the culture is influencing our marriage, I will take one of the following steps (check one):

   ☐ Evaluate the impact of my time with the television's remote control.

   ☐ Decide if what I feed my thinking (whatever media sources come into my mind) is positive or negative about marriage.

   ☐ Discuss with my spouse what each of our friends likely value in marriage. Do we share the same values?

☐ Because different expectations about financial issues have been a threat to our marriage, I will take one of the following actions:

   ☐ Assume responsibility for paying the bills

   ☐ Discuss (as a couple) our financial status at least once a month

   ☐ Make an appointment to get financial help

COUPLE APPLICATION

Let's talk! We will discuss:

☐ Specific ways we believe the culture has negatively influenced our marriage

☐ Specific ways the homes in which we were raised have had an effect on our marriage

☐ Expectations we feel from one another

☐ If either of us is in danger of having an affair (Review the list on page 40.)

Let's learn! We will read the following book together:

☐ *Starting Your Marriage Right* by Dennis and Barbara Rainey (great for couples who are newly married)

☐ *The Seven Conflicts: Resolving The Most Common Disagreements In Marriage* by Tim and Joy Downs (love your spouse and have a great marriage in spite of conflict)

☐ *Little House on the Freeway* by Tim and Darcy Kimmel (great for couples where life is over scheduled)

3

God's Purposes
for Oneness

God's Purposes for Oneness

Session 3 Overview

Understanding God's purposes for marriage leads a couple toward oneness.

Introduction

A. Consider the question: "Why marriage?"

B. Why should we use the Bible as our guide to experiencing oneness?

C. Marriage is God's idea.

   1. God designed marriage to be a lifetime __commitment__ between one man and one woman.

   2. God designed marriage as the __first__ social institution in life.

   3. God designed marriage to be the first system of __interdependent__ relationships.

   4. God designed the marriage relationship as the __priority__ relationship of the family. (not the kids)

D. God's design for __oneness__ in marriage is at the heart of God's purpose for mankind.

1. Oneness can be defined as "being in joyful
   ___*agreement*___ with God's will and purposes."

2. Oneness is to be experienced on two levels:

   a. Vertically with God
   b. Horizontally with each other

I. Purpose No. 1: Mirror God's image

And God created humanity in His own image ... male and female He created them.

Genesis 1:27

A. God made humanity to mirror His image on Planet Earth.

B. God made two distinctly different humans (male and female) so
   that ___*together*___ they would reflect the image of God.

1. Their oneness reflects the character and unity of God (Matthew 19:4-6; John 17:22-23).

2. Their oneness is a living picture of the intimate relationship between Jesus Christ and His followers (Ephesians 5:22-33).

C. Couples who mirror God's image experience oneness with their
   ___*creator*___.

II. Purpose No. 2: Mutually complete one another (to experience companionship)

Then the Lord God said, "It is not good for the man to be alone; I will make him a helper suitable for him."

Genesis 2:18

A. ___Companiowship___ replaces isolation.

1. To mutually complete one another means to create

   something ___together___ that does not exist apart.

2. Self-centered individuality destroys oneness and companionship.

B. Companionship in marriage is God's provision to meet our deep longing for close, intimate relationships.

C. Couples who mutually complete one another experience oneness

   with ___Each___ ___other___ .

III. Purpose No. 3: Multiply a godly legacy

And God blessed them; and God said to them, "Be fruitful and multiply, and fill the earth."

Genesis 1:28a

A. God created men and women as His ___ambassador___ who would glorify Him on earth.

B. Marriage provides the divine ___context___ for having children.

C. Oneness in marriage is necessary in order to ___multiply___ a godly legacy.

1. Neither women or men are made emotionally, spiritually, or physically to raise children by themselves. Child rearing requires a ___team___ effort.

2. To appreciate their sexual identity, children must see a harmonious marriage modeled by their parents.

3. The roles of husband and wife are best understood by children as their parents model a harmonious marriage in the home.

4. The best hope for children to understand unconditional love comes as parents demonstrate that kind of love in the home.

D. Couples who multiply a godly legacy experience oneness with their ___children___.

IV. God's purposes for marriage are challenged by an opposing force.

A. From the beginning, the Scriptures state that ___Satan___ has challenged God and His purposes for marriage.

B. Satan's opposition is focused on ___independence___ from God.

   1. The basis of his opposition was pride. Pride says, "I will do it myself." (Isaiah 14:12-14, Ezekiel 28:12-18)

   2. Earth became the battlefield for a spiritual war.

C. God created mankind and placed them in the ___middle___ of this spiritual battle.

Now the serpent was more crafty than any beast of the field which the Lord God had made. And he said to the woman, "Indeed, has God said, 'You shall not eat from any tree of the garden'?" And the woman said to the serpent, "From the fruit of the trees of the garden we may eat; but from the fruit of the tree which is in the middle of the garden, God has said, 'You shall not eat from it or touch it, lest you die.'"

And the serpent said to the woman, "You surely shall not die! For God knows that in the day you eat from it your eyes will be opened, and you will be like God, knowing good and evil." When the woman saw that the tree was good for food, and that it was a delight to the eyes, and that the tree was desirable to make one wise, she took from its fruit and ate; and she gave also to her husband with her, and he ate.

Genesis 3:1-6

D. Because mankind willfully chose independence from God, there have been at least three consequences man has suffered throughout history.

   1. The image of God in humanity has been defaced.

For all have sinned and fall short of the glory of God.

Romans 3:23

2. Marital companionship has been threatened by:

   a. Shame, guilt, and fear

   Then the eyes of both of them were opened, and they knew that they were naked; and they sewed fig leaves together and made themselves loin coverings. And they heard the sound of the LORD God walking in the garden in the cool of the day, and the man and his wife hid themselves from the presence of the LORD God among the trees of the garden. Then the LORD God called to the man, and said to him, "Where are you?" And he said, "I heard the sound of Thee in the garden, and I was afraid because I was naked; so I hid myself."

   Genesis 3:7-10

   b. Blame shifting

   And the man said, "The woman that Thou gavest to be with me, she gave me from the tree, and I ate." Then the LORD God said to the woman, "What is this you have done?" And the woman said, "The serpent deceived me, and I ate."

   Genesis 3:12-13

   c. Battle for control

   To the woman He [God] said, " ... your desire shall be for your husband, and he shall rule over you."

   Genesis 3:16

3. A godly legacy has been challenged by a godless legacy.

   And it came about when they (Cain and Abel) were in the field that Cain rose up against his brother and killed him.

   Genesis 4:8

E. Satan's power is threatened by couples who are becoming one; therefore Satan concentrates his major ___attacks___ on them.

For our struggle is not against flesh and blood, but against the rulers, against the powers, against the world forces of this darkness, against the spiritual forces of wickedness in the heavenly places.

Ephesians 6:12

V. Summary

A. Marriage is far more important than you may have thought.

   1. Marriage reflects God's image on Planet Earth.

   2. Marriage is designed for a husband and wife to mutually complete each other.

   3. Marriage is designed to multiply a godly legacy.

B. Recognize that your marriage is taking place on a spiritual battlefield, not on a romantic balcony.

   1. God's purposes reveal that our spouse is not our enemy.

   2. God's purposes can be accomplished by following His plan.

   3. God's Word demands a response: Will you commit to fulfilling His purposes for your marriage?

Session Four

God's Plan for Oneness

God's Plan for Oneness

Session 4 Overview

Oneness is discovered as we receive our spouse as a gift from God.

[handwritten: 1957 song who, who wrote the book of love — God]

Introduction

- The world's pattern for marriage has obviously failed.

- What is God's plan to accomplish His purposes for marriage?

- God's plan for oneness in marriage involves three responsibilities: You must leave, cleave, and become one flesh.

  [handwritten: commit]

I. LEAVE: The first responsibility is to establish independence from your parents.

For this cause a man shall leave his father and his mother ...

Genesis 2:24a

A. Leaving must be done in the context of honor to one's parents.

B. Beware of overdependence on parents.

[handwritten: stand on own 2 first s are responsible for self; I love me & I choose to love you if you don't like me, I'm not shattered; interdependent — independent but chose to need the other]

Commit
sticking like glue

II. CLEAVE: The second responsibility is to establish commitment to one another.

For this cause a man shall leave his father and his mother and shall cleave to his wife ...

Genesis 2:24

I'm so miserable without you it almost seems like your here.

A. Revisiting the garden illustrates this principle of cleaving to your spouse.

my best friend ran off, with my wife, I miss him

1. God created Adam with an unmet need: Adam was alone.

no one cares (Jr. high dance)
no one to love me

4

Then the Lord God said, "It is not good for the man to be alone; I will make him a helper suitable for him."

Genesis 2:18

a. Up to this point in creation, God had said everything was good.

b. Adam had several advantages over modern man.

c. God chose to build a unique need into Adam that was not met by God's personal presence alone. need for companionship

until you recognize your aloneness, you don't know your need for companionship.

2. God showed Adam his NEED.

And out of the ground the Lord God formed every beast of the field and every bird of the sky, and brought them to the man to see what he would call them; and whatever the man called a living creature, that was its name. And the man gave names to all the cattle, and to the birds of the sky, and to every beast of the field, but for Adam there was not found a helper suitable for him.

Genesis 2:19-20

helper – suitable one
give assistance to, coming to the aide
help to see life from diff. perspective
someone to meet your gaps

a. God gave Adam the assignment of naming all the animals.

b. Adam saw his own need as he named the animals.

c. There was "not found a helper suitable" for Adam.

3. God ___provided___ for Adam's need by creating Eve.

So the Lord God caused a deep sleep to fall upon the man, and he slept; then He took one of his ribs, and closed up the flesh at that place. And the Lord God fashioned into a woman the rib which He had taken from the man, and brought her to the man.

Genesis 2:21-22

    a. God fashioned Eve to be suitable for Adam.

    b. God presented Eve to Adam.

    c. An important question was, would Adam receive Eve?

B. Adam's perspective of God enabled him to ___see___ Eve as God's perfect provision for him.

And the man said, "This is now bone of my bones, and flesh of my flesh; she shall be called woman, because she was taken out of man."

Genesis 2:23

He was pumped!

1. In this passage, God illustrates a cornerstone principle for marriage: We must ___chose___ ___to___ receive our spouse as God's perfect provision for us.

    a. We must focus on God's ___character___ and His ___goodness___ in providing our spouse.

    b. Our acceptance of our spouse is NOT based on our spouse's performance.

2. Adam enthusiastically received Eve because he knew and trusted God, not because of Eve's performance.

are we able to receive our spouse as
God's gift to us.
Recognize aloneness + realize need. God's plan — gift of
didn't earn it   spouse

My spouse is God's gift to me.

III. Hindrances to Reception: Three barriers make it difficult to receive our spouse as a gift from God.

A. Our natural _____ .

men & women are just different - created that way but does create barriers

DIFFERENCES

Gender
Perspectives
Temperaments
Backgrounds
Preferences
Roles

And God created man in His own image, in the image of God He created him; male and female He created them.

Genesis 1:27

1. Differences are not ___hinderances___ to achieving God's purposes in your marriage.

2. Differences are God's ___tools___ to teach us to trust Him and His goodness.

Iron sharpens iron, so one man sharpens another.

Proverbs 27:17

B. Our natural ___WEAKNESS___ .

1. Weaknesses are not ___justifications___ for rejecting our spouse.

2. Weaknesses have divine purposes in our lives.

WEAKNESSES

Impatient
Indecisive
Overly Talkative
Disorganized
Critical Spirit
Demanding

C. Our natural ___Self centeredness___.

1. We must ___admit___ that we are selfish.

2. Receiving our spouse is demonstrated by ___placing___ our spouse's needs ahead of our own.

Do nothing from selfishness or empty conceit, but with humility of mind let each of you regard one another as more important than himself.

Philippians 2:3

D. To reject your spouse in any way is to:

1. Reject God and His provision for your life

2. Reflect negatively on the character of God

3. Demonstrate unbelief and disobedience toward God

4. Fail to fulfill God's plan and purposes for marriage

E. God uses our natural differences, weaknesses, and selfishness to build oneness.

F. As an act of your will, you must ___receive___ (not just accept) your spouse as God's gift made personally for you to meet your specific aloneness needs.

my spouse needs my unconditional acceptance

IV. BECOME ONE FLESH: The third responsibility is to establish intimacy with one another.

physical intimacy

For this cause a man shall leave his father and his mother and shall cleave to his wife and they shall become one flesh.

Genesis 2:24

A. Physical intimacy is the expression of complete oneness (body and soul) in marriage.

B. The result of leaving, cleaving, and becoming one flesh is _____transparency_____ with one another or oneness (naked and not ashamed).

And the man and his wife were both naked and were not ashamed.

Genesis 2:25

C. "One flesh" intimacy is built on a foundation of _____sacrificial_____ love for each other.

D. Will you choose to look to God as the Giver of good gifts and receive your spouse as His perfect gift for you?

Every good thing bestowed and every perfect gift is from above, coming down from the Father of lights, with whom there is no variation, or shifting shadow.

James 1:17

V. Summary

A. Our perspective of God enables us to receive our spouse as His gift.

   1. Is God big enough to make the best out of your worst situations?

   2. Will you trust God as Adam did?

B. Remember: The basis for one's reception of his spouse is faith in God's integrity. It is impossible to trust the character and integrity of someone you do not know!

C. Relying on God's power is the key to fulfilling God's purposes and plan for marriage.

Clint Black

God's Purposes and Plan for Marriage

Application Project

This application project has two sections: the individual section and the interaction section. Be sure to leave adequate time to interact as a couple on the interaction section.

 Individual Section

25 Minutes

Setting: Find a place to be alone, but near your spouse, to complete this section.

Objective: To surface and identify your true feelings toward each other.

Instructions: Spend time in prayer individually in Part One and then complete Part Two.

Part One: (10 Minutes) Spend time in prayer.

1. Confess to God any rejection of, withdrawal from, or bitterness toward your spouse as sin. Thank God for His forgiveness and the cleansing blood of Christ.

    If we confess our sins, He is faithful and righteous to forgive us our sins and to cleanse us from all unrighteousness.

   1 John 1:9

2. Commit to God totally, by faith, to receive your spouse based upon the integrity and sovereignty of God. Be sure to put this commitment in your love letter.

3. Commit to God to trust Him with your spouse's differences and weaknesses and to love your spouse unconditionally with Christ's love (apart from performance). Be certain you put this commitment in your love letter.

4. Tell God you are willing to let Him change you through both your spouse's strengths as well as your spouse's weaknesses, differences, and selfishness.

Part Two: (15 Minutes)

Write out the answers to the following questions in the form of a love letter. Use the blank Love Letter on pages 64-65 for your letter.

1. What were the qualities that attracted me the most to you when we first met?

> Easy to talk too
> had similar values
> we liked to do many similar things
> liked to have fun

2. What qualities do I appreciate or have learned to appreciate most about you since we have been married?

> positive or optimistic attitude
> level headedness
> appreciate you time helping the kids to learn (book)
> appreciate your becoming electronics expert

3. How have our differences helped me grow spiritually and emotionally?

> Your strong committment to God has strenghtewed mine
> (especially in korea)
> I did not like kids before we were married, but
> because of you I do now ~~appreciate~~ see them as
> a blessing and not a burden.

4. What steps will I commit to take to love God and you more?

> Recognize that I need you and that you
> are God's gift to me and then is a no return policy.

Interaction Section

15 Minutes

Setting: Get together with your spouse and complete this section. Make sure you can talk freely.

Objective: To share your feelings and commitment with each other.

Instructions: Read each question and spend time sharing.

1. Share and discuss your letter.

2. Verbalize to your spouse the commitment you made to God during your individual prayer time.

3. Close your time together by taking turns thanking God for each other.

4. Write the points of action you will take individually, as a couple, and with others on the *Take It Home* page.

5. Then, record that point of action you most want to apply on the *Take It Home Summary* flap attached to the back cover.

Love Letter

4

Love Letter

Dear George

When we met, there were many things that attracted me to you. You were very easy to talk to and we liked many of the same activities/events. You liked to have fun, and the things you thought were fun were my idea of fun too. However, I really liked the fact that you had strong values and you lived your life according to those values.

Since we've been married I've come to appreciate some of your other qualities. You seem to have a positive and optimistic attitude about most things. Sometimes I only see the negative, but you turn it around for me. You also have a level headedness about you and sometimes we need that. You have a teaching strength and have the patience to work with the kids. You help them to grow in ways that I can't.

Your strong commitment to God has straightened mine, especially when we were in Korea. I am stronger in my faith because of you. Also, as you may remember, I wasn't sure I wanted kids to be part of my life. You changed that. I now see kids as a blessing and not a burden.

For a long time now, we have not had a oneness in our marriage. I did not see you as God's gift to me. Your performance was required for my performance. I will now try with God's help to love you as God's gift that I need. There's a no return policy on this gift. I will commit to trying to gain oneness and bring the romance back to our marriage.

Love, Brenda

Take It Home

INDIVIDUAL APPLICATION

 I will do this! Check one or more of the following:

☐ This week, I will go back and read the following passages from the Bible in one sitting: Genesis 1-3, Ephesians 5, Colossians 3, 1 Peter 3, Titus 2.

☐ At the next break, I will tell my spouse "You are not my enemy."

☐ For husbands, I will begin praying with my wife on a daily basis.

☐ As a tangible way of receiving my spouse as God's perfect provision for me, I will:

   ☐ Tell my spouse this weekend that I am thankful that God brought us together.

   ☐ Ask forgiveness (from God and from my spouse) for how I have rejected my spouse in the past.

   ☐ Make a fresh commitment to God and to my spouse that our marriage will reflect God's image.

☐ Recognizing that the best thing I can do for my children is to love my spouse, I will tell my children this week that I love their mother or father very much, and that our marriage comes first, ahead of them. (This is a key action point for couples in blended families.)

☐ I will specifically affirm my spouse for the differences that may have irritated me in the past. I will look for the hidden strengths in those things I have seen as weaknesses.

COUPLE APPLICATION

 Let's talk! We will discuss:

☐ Ways we can cultivate companionship in our relationship. We can choose a common interest to begin to pursue together.

☐ Ways I have seen Satan work in our relationship

☐ Areas in our marriage where we may still be dependent on our parents

☐ Our view of the value of children in a family—either having or adopting children (if we are currently childless), whether we have unwittingly adopted a cultural view about the value of children, and the number of children we ought to have

☐ Taking a planning weekend sometime in the next three months to review the material from this weekend

☐ Examine our family priorities in light of God's plan for marriage

 Let's learn! We will read the following book together:

☐ *Two Becoming One* by Don and Sally Meredith (for couples to go deeper in understanding God's plan and purposes for marriage)

☐ *Rocking the Roles* (for couples who want to understand the unique differences between men and women in marriage)

☐ *Intimate Allies* by Dan Allender

☐ *Sacred Marriage* by Gary Thomas

Session Five

5

Preparation for Marriage

Preparation for Marriage

Session 5 Overview

Making right choices before marriage promotes oneness in marriage.

Introduction

- Marriage is a decision that will change the rest of your life.

- Engagement is a time to:

    —Begin to develop the skills you'll need for a successful marriage.

    —Continue to evaluate your compatibility as a couple.

    —Prepare for future intimacy and commitment.

I. Evaluating your compatibility

A. An engaged couple must continue to evaluate whether they are right for each other.

    1. A couple must continue to ask a series of practical questions:

        a. How much are we really alike?

        b. Do we agree on the basic plan for our future marriage?

        c. Do we agree that divorce is not an option?

        d. Do either of us have any unaddressed personal problems that could cause difficulty in our future marriage?

        e. Do we agree on our attitudes toward making and spending money?

        f. How do we talk, fight, and make decisions together?

    2. A couple must be willing to ask some hard questions about their relationship. How much has our decision to get married been affected by:

        • Feelings?

        • Outside pressures?

        • Fear that this may be our last chance?

        • Fear of being disgraced if we break our engagement?

B. An engaged couple must also evaluate their spiritual compatibility.

    1. Are we committed to something greater than our marriage?

    2. Do we have the same essential spiritual beliefs?

5

Therefore if there is any encouragement in Christ, if there is any consolation of love, if there is any fellowship of the Spirit, if any affection and compassion, make my joy complete by being of the same mind, maintaining the same love, united in spirit, intent on one purpose.

Philippians 2:1-2

3. Do we have similar levels of interest in spiritual things?

C. An engaged couple should consider outside guidance.

1. The Bible is a source of wisdom and direction.

Your word is a lamp to my feet and a light to my path.

Psalm 119:105

2. Prayer is a source of guidance and confidence.

Trust in the Lord with all your heart and do not lean on your own understanding. In all your ways acknowledge Him, and He will make your paths straight.

Proverbs 3:5-6

3. The advice of wise counselors can give you an objective perspective on your relationship.

- Parents

- Close friends

- A pastor

- A professional counselor

Where there is no guidance the people fall, but in abundance of counselors there is victory.

Proverbs 11:14

4. A couple may need help in confirming their decision to marry.

II. Preparing for future intimacy and commitment

A. The Bible instructs couples to save sexual involvement until marriage for a variety of practical reasons.

Marriage is to be held in honor among all, and the marriage bed is to be undefiled ...

Hebrews 13:4a

1. The ability to demonstrate sexual self-control now lays a foundation for future trust and intimacy.

   a. Sexual self-control is necessary throughout married life.

   b. Couples who are sexually active before marriage may have a higher incidence of affairs after marriage.

   c. Couples who live together before marriage may have a higher incidence of divorce.

2. Sex during the engagement period can "cloud" more significant issues.

   a. Sex before marriage can create a false sense of compatibility.

   b. The emotional power of a sexual relationship can keep a couple from thinking clearly and objectively.

3. Sex during the engagement period can replace communication rather than enhance it.

B. An engaged couple may need to discuss how to wait until marriage to have sex.

C. Every engaged couple should invest in their future security by agreeing together to keep the Purity Covenant until they're married.

III. Summary

A. Engagement is not marriage.

B. Engagement is a time to make sure you are ready for marriage and a time to lay a good foundation for the future.

C. Remember: It's easier to break off an engagement than a marriage.

5

The Purity Covenant

Get alone together. Sit face to face and hold hands. Begin by having the man read the Scripture passage below. Then the man is to read the promise of purity to his fiancée. Next the woman is to read the promise to the man. Finally, pray and both of you should make your commitment to God.

1 Thessalonians 4:3-8

For this is the will of God, your sanctification; that is, that you abstain from sexual immorality; that each of you know how to possess his own vessel in sanctification and honor, not in lustful passion, like the Gentiles who do not know God; and that no man transgress and defraud his brother in the matter because the Lord is the avenger in all these things, just as we also told you before and solemnly warned you. For God has not called us for the purpose of impurity, but in sanctification. Consequently, he who rejects this is not rejecting man but the God who gives His Holy Spirit to you.

1 Corinthians 6:18-20

Flee immorality. Every other sin that a man commits is outside the body, but the immoral man sins against his own body. Or do you not know that your body is a temple of the Holy Spirit who is in you, whom you have from God, and that you are not your own? For you have been bought with a price: therefore glorify God in your body.

Acts 24:16

In view of this, I also do my best to maintain always a blameless conscience both before God and before men.

Promise of Purity

◆ In obedience to God's command, I promise to protect your moral purity from this day until our honeymoon.

◆ Because I respect and honor you, I commit to build up the inner person of your heart rather than violate you.

◆ I pledge to show my love for you in ways that allow both of us to maintain a clear conscience before God and each other.

Signed _____ Date _____

Signed _____ Date _____

Preparation for Marriage: Engaged Couples

Application Project

This application project has two sections: the individual section and the interaction section. Be sure to leave adequate time to interact as a couple on the interaction section.

Individual Section
No Time Limit

Setting: Stay together and complete this section. For fun, keep the results of this section and review them after one year of marriage.

Objective: To find out how well you know each other and to galvanize your commitment to one another.

Instructions: Without interaction, complete the chart below. (No cheating, please!) Put an X on the number that best describes you on each quality or trait. Circle the number that best describes your fiancé/fiancée. Be truthful. When both are finished, discuss your answers.

Disciplined	1	2	3	4	5	6	7	8	9	10	Impulsive
Stubborn	1	2	3	4	5	6	7	8	9	10	Flexible
Aggressive/Assertive	1	2	3	4	5	6	7	8	9	10	Compliant/Passive
Infatuated Love	1	2	3	4	5	6	7	8	9	10	Realistic Love
Task-Oriented	1	2	3	4	5	6	7	8	9	10	People-Oriented
Center of God's Will	1	2	3	4	5	6	7	8	9	10	Out of God's Will
Pessimistic	1	2	3	4	5	6	7	8	9	10	Optimistic
Outgoing	1	2	3	4	5	6	7	8	9	10	Withdrawn
High Expectations About Marriage	1	2	3	4	5	6	7	8	9	10	Low Expectations About Marriage
Sympathetic	1	2	3	4	5	6	7	8	9	10	Insensitive
Decisive	1	2	3	4	5	6	7	8	9	10	Indecisive
Tense	1	2	3	4	5	6	7	8	9	10	Relaxed
Spendthrift	1	2	3	4	5	6	7	8	9	10	Scrooge
Emotionally Open	1	2	3	4	5	6	7	8	9	10	Emotionally Closed
Good Self-Image	1	2	3	4	5	6	7	8	9	10	Poor Self-Image
Critical	1	2	3	4	5	6	7	8	9	10	Gracious
Growing Spiritually	1	2	3	4	5	6	7	8	9	10	Spiritually Stagnant
Heart for God	1	2	3	4	5	6	7	8	9	10	Lukewarm to God
Idealistic	1	2	3	4	5	6	7	8	9	10	Realistic
Openly Affectionate	1	2	3	4	5	6	7	8	9	10	Reserved with Affection

Interaction Section

No Time Limit

Setting: This is the time for serious, personal reflection on the insights you gained from the individual section. This is to be done in complete privacy.

Objective: To seriously evaluate your relationship in terms of how well you, as a couple, are suited for marriage.

1. Does the individual section cause you to question God's leading toward marriage?   Yes   No
   If yes, why?

2. Are you willing to receive this person with all of their strengths and weaknesses as God's personal provision for you?

3. What steps of action should you take in light of your previous answer?

4. Write one point of action you will take individually, as a couple, or with others on the *Take It Home* page.

5. Then, record that point of action onto the *Take It Home Summary* flap attached to the back cover.

6. Schedule a time to confirm God's will for your relationship by completing the post-conference project on the next page.

7. Very Important: Schedule your one-year, 10,000 mile marriage tune-up for the next Weekend to Remember Conference. We promise you will hear more the next time.

Preparation for Marriage:
Pre-Engaged Couples
Application Project

This application project has two sections: the individual section and the interaction section. Be sure to leave adequate time to interact as a couple on the interaction section.

Individual Section

Post Conference

Setting: This project should be done completely alone. Schedule a private place, away from distractions, where you can pray, study God's Word, think, and work without interruption. It is imperative that you spend this time away from each other.

Objective: To discern God's will for marriage.

Instructions:

1. Schedule two days, probably a weekend. Be sure to include at least one night to "sleep on your decision."
2. Spend time with God in prayer and reading His Word. The Psalms and Proverbs are great to help prepare your heart.
3. Review your Weekend to Remember Conference notebook. Special review should be given to the messages "God's Purposes for Oneness" and "God's Plan for Oneness."
4. Use this checklist to remember to take the following:
   - ❑ Bible
   - ❑ Notebook/paper/pen
   - ❑ Audio series: "Are You Ready? Becoming Mr. or Mrs. Right" FamilyLife ID #790
   - ❑ Weekend to Remember Conference notebook
   - ❑ A prayerful heart

Part One

Pray and work your way through these six steps from the conference message on God's will. Then complete the seventh step.

Step 1: Are you right with God? Confess your sins and humble yourself before God. Relinquish all rights to your life to God. Read Romans 12:1-2 and Psalm 90:11-12.

> *If I regard wickedness in my heart, the Lord will not hear.*
>
> Psalm 66:18

Step 2: Write down 10 reasons you think your partner is the one you should marry.

1.

2.

3.

4.

5.

6.

7.

8.

9.

10.

Step 3: Write 10 reasons this is the time in your life that you should marry.

1.

2.

3.

4.

5.

6.

7.

8.

9.

10.

5

Step 4: Answer the following questions:

    a. Do you both have a heart for God?

    b. Is Jesus Christ at the center of your relationship?

    c. Are you both pursuing God?

    d. Are your philosophies compatible?

    e. Are your goals and plans for the future compatible?

    f. Can you accept your personality differences?

    g. Are you emotionally compatible? Are there presently any areas of your emotional relationship which remain uncomfortable, difficult to discuss, or which cause regular conflict?

    h. What are others saying about your relationship?

    i. What would be most difficult about ending this relationship right now?

    j. Can you live without this person?

    k. Are you willing to commit yourself to this person unconditionally for the rest of your life?

Step 5: Write out a list of your fears.

Step 6: Confess or acknowledge them to God. Read 1 John 1:9.

Step 7: Commit to God to accept or reject the other as God's provision for your needs. Can you receive that person just as he is right now?

Step 8: Write out the commitment to God. If you cannot receive him as God's provision, then write out a resolution to God that releases that other person from the relationship.

Step 9: Hold your decision privately for 24 hours allowing God to confirm it with His conviction that you are to marry. Continue to pray during this time allowing God to give you freedom to move forward. Do not move forward in the relationship without God's peace! God's peace is only found in two right relationships: vertically with God and horizontally with others. Read Philippians 4:4-9.

Part Two

Make your decision known as you complete steps eight and nine from the conference message on God's purposes.

Step 1: Tell one close friend, which allows him to confirm your decision and to hold you accountable. It is very important that you continue to be accountable to a friend after you make your decision. After you have verbalized your decision (Step 8) do not back down on your commitment without first discussing it with your friend.

Step 2: Verbalize your decision to your potential spouse.

Part Three

Very Important. Schedule your one-year, 10,000 mile marriage tune-up for the next Weekend to Remember Conference. We promise you will hear more the next time.

Step 1: Write one point of action you will take immediately, as a couple, or with others on the *Take It Home Summary* flap on the back cover.

Step 2: Then, record that Take It Home action onto the *Take It Home Summary* flap attached to the back cover.

Take It Home

INDIVIDUAL APPLICATION

 I will do this! Check one or more of the following:

☐ I will think again about my fiancé's/fiancée's spiritual beliefs and interest in spiritual things to determine if we are essentially compatible in this critical area.

☐ I will pray about and answer the following questions this week:

  • Can I live without this partner?

  • Am I able to unconditionally accept this partner with no agenda for change?

☐ I will ask friends who know both of us if they have any reservations about our plans to be married.

☐ MEN: I will begin now taking the initiative to pray every day with my fiancé/fiancée, as a pattern for our coming marriage.

☐ I will sign the Purity Covenant found on page 73. I will remain sexually pure from this point until after our wedding.

COUPLE APPLICATION

 Let's talk! We will discuss:

☐ Any doubts or concerns with which we are still struggling and determine their significance

☐ Whether we agree that divorce will not be an option in our marriage

☐ Issues from our past that we may need to be open and honest about with each other

☐ Money—What do we believe about debt, giving, etc.

 Let's learn! We will read the following book together:

☐ *Preparing For Marriage* by Dave Boehi, Brent Nelson, Jeff Schulte, and Lloyd Shadrach (great for discussing many of the important questions engaged couples face.)

☐ *Starting Your Marriage Right* by Dennis and Barbara Rainey

Session Six

6

God's Power
for Oneness

God's Power for Oneness

Session 6 Overview

God's power is experienced by knowing God and by growing in our relationship with Him.

Introduction

- For those who seek it, God provides the power necessary to fulfill His purposes and to carry out His plan for oneness.

- We experience this power by knowing God and allowing His Spirit to control our lives by faith.

I. Knowing God personally

A. God loves you and created you for a <u>relationship</u> **with Him.**

1. God loves you.

    For God so loved the world, that He gave His only begotten Son, that whoever believes in Him should not perish, but have eternal life.

   John 3:16

2. God wants you to know Him.

    And this is eternal life, that they may know Thee, the only true God, and Jesus Christ whom Thou hast sent.

   John 17:3

What prevents us from knowing God personally?

B. Humanity is ___*separated*___ from God and cannot know Him personally or experience His love and power.

1. All of us are sinful. a. *inability*
   b. *willful choice (decision)*

> For all have sinned and fall short of the glory of God.
>
> Romans 3:23

Eternal death

HOLY GOD

eternal life

2. Our sin separates us from God.

(earn)
> For the wages of sin is death ...
>
> Romans 6:23a

How can the gulf between God and man be bridged?

C. Jesus Christ is God's only provision for our sin. Through Him alone we can know God personally and experience His love.

1. God became a man in the Person of Jesus Christ.

> The Word (God) became flesh and made his dwelling among us. We have seen his glory, the glory of the One and Only, who came from the Father, full of grace and truth.
>
> John 1:14

2. He ___died___ in our place.

But God demonstrates His own love toward us, in that while we were yet sinners, Christ died for us.

Romans 5:8

3. He ___rose___ from the dead.

Christ died for our sins ... He was buried ... He was raised on the third day according to the Scriptures ... He appeared to Peter, then to the twelve. After that He appeared to more than five hundred ...

1 Corinthians 15:3-6

4. He is the ___only___ way to God.

Jesus said to him, "I am the way, and the truth, and the life; no one comes to the Father, but through Me."

John 14:6

D. We must individually ___receive___ Jesus Christ as Savior and Lord; then we can know God personally and experience His love.

1. We must change our minds about the way we have lived.

2. We must receive Christ by accepting the free gift of salvation He offers us.

But as many as received Him, to them He gave the right to become children of God, even to those who believe in His name.

John 1:12

For by grace you have been saved through faith; and that not of yourselves, it is the gift of God; not as a result of works, that no one should boast.

Ephesians 2:8-9

Self-Directed Life

Christ-Directed Life

E. **What are the results of placing my faith in Jesus Christ? The Bible says:**

1. My sins are _____forgiven_____ (Colossians 2:13).

2. I possess the gift of _____Eternal_____ life.

 And the witness is this, that God has given us eternal life, and this life is in His Son ...

1 John 5:11

3. I have been given the ____holy____ ____spirit____ to empower me to pursue intimacy with God and oneness with my spouse.

F. **I can respond to God right now by faith through prayer.**

A suggested life-changing decision: "Lord Jesus, I need You. Thank You for dying on the cross for my sins. I acknowledge that I am a sinner and I am separated from You. Please forgive me. I receive You as my Savior and Lord. Thank You for forgiving my sins and giving me eternal life. Please take control of my life. Make me the kind of person You want me to be."

Signature _Brenda Chuning-Kulech_ Date _19 Feb 05_

II. Experiencing the power of God

A. To experience the power of God in my marriage, I must:

1. Listen to God (study His Word)

   • Read it

   • Hear it taught

   • Meditate on it

   • Memorize it

2. Talk to God (prayer)

3. Develop relationships with other believers (the church)

4. Tell others about God

5. Understand Who the Holy Spirit is and how I can experience His power in my life

B. Who is the Holy Spirit?

1. He is _____God_____ . He is the third Person of the Trinity, co-equal with the Father and the Son.

2. He is our Helper and Comforter.

3. He is the Christian's source of power to live a consistent lifestyle of love and obedience.

C. What does the Holy Spirit do in our lives?

1. He ___teaches___ us how to live by guiding us to truth.

"But the Helper, the Holy Spirit, whom the Father will send in My name, He will teach you all things, and will bring to your remembrance all that I said to you."

John 14:26

2. He ___convicts___ us of the presence of sin in our lives.

And He, when He comes, will convict the world concerning sin, and righteousness and judgment.

John 16:8

3. He helps us forgive each other.

And do not grieve the Holy Spirit of God, by whom you were sealed for the day of redemption. Let all bitterness and wrath and anger and clamor and slander be put away from you, along with all malice. And be kind to one another, tenderhearted, forgiving each other, just as God in Christ also has forgiven you.

Ephesians 4:30-32

4. He helps us love each other unconditionally.

D. What does it mean to be controlled by the Holy Spirit?

1. The Bible describes this control as "being filled with the Spirit."

And do not get drunk with wine, for that is dissipation, but be filled with the Spirit.

Ephesians 5:18

2. It does not mean you get more of God. It means He gets more of you.

3. It means allowing the Holy Spirit ___unhindered___ control of my life.

4. It means the fruit of the Holy Spirit will begin to be evident.

But the fruit of the Spirit is love, joy, peace, patience, kindness, goodness, faithfulness, gentleness, self-control; against such things there is no law.

Galatians 5:22-23

E. Which side of the following diagram best represents my life? Put a check by the appropriate side.

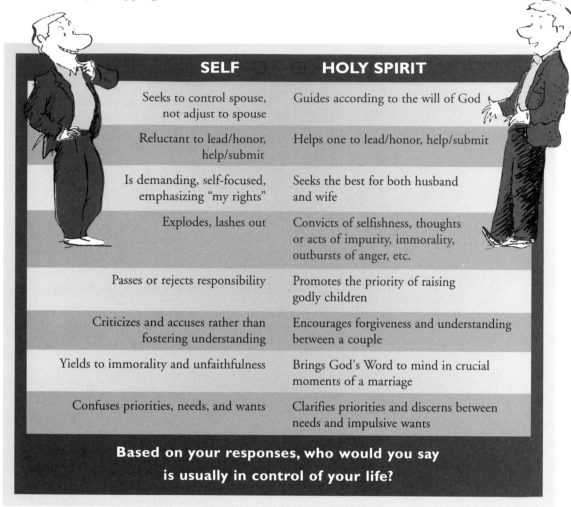

SELF ☐	☐ HOLY SPIRIT
Seeks to control spouse, not adjust to spouse	Guides according to the will of God
Reluctant to lead/honor, help/submit	Helps one to lead/honor, help/submit
Is demanding, self-focused, emphasizing "my rights"	Seeks the best for both husband and wife
Explodes, lashes out	Convicts of selfishness, thoughts or acts of impurity, immorality, outbursts of anger, etc.
Passes or rejects responsibility	Promotes the priority of raising godly children
Criticizes and accuses rather than fostering understanding	Encourages forgiveness and understanding between a couple
Yields to immorality and unfaithfulness	Brings God's Word to mind in crucial moments of a marriage
Confuses priorities, needs, and wants	Clarifies priorities and discerns between needs and impulsive wants

**Based on your responses, who would you say
is usually in control of your life?**

F. How can I be filled (controlled and empowered) with the Holy Spirit?

1. I must ___desire___ to be filled. (It is God's will for you.)

2. I ___confess___ and turn away from any known sin.

*If we confess our sins, He is faithful and righteous to forgive us
our sins and to cleanse us from all unrighteousness.*

1 John 1:9

3. I ___surrender___ those areas I have kept from Him.

4. I must regularly pray for His power in my life.

G. How can I experience the Holy Spirit's power day by day in my marriage?

1. Enjoy times together reading God's Word.

2. Practice praying together.

3. Spend time in fellowship together with other believers.

4. When sin occurs, confess and turn from it.

A suggested life-changing decision: Dear Father, I confess that I have been seeking to control my own life, and as a result, I have sinned against You. Please forgive me. I want You to have unhindered control of all my life. Please fill me with Your Holy Spirit and help me surrender complete control of my life to You. As an expression of my faith, I now thank You for directing my life and filling me with the Holy Spirit. In Jesus' name. Amen.

Signature ___Burda Churring-luled___ Date ___19 Feb 05___

Christian's
bar of
soap

III. Summary

A. Understand that being controlled and empowered by the Holy Spirit is an ongoing and continual process.

B. As we surrender the control of our lives to God, we can begin to fulfill His purposes and plan for marriage.

C. We will experience oneness (harmony) in our marriage.

Take It Home

I will do this! Check one or more of the following:

☐ If I checked either box (to receive Christ as my Lord and Savior, or to be filled with the Holy Spirit) I will find someone this week whom I respect as a Christian and ask him what I ought to do next.

☐ I will commit to be an active part of a local church where the Bible is clearly taught. If not currently a member of a local church, I will commit to look for a place where we can worship together each week.

☐ I will read one book from the New Testament each month for a year, beginning with the Gospel of John.

☐ I will follow a plan to read completely through the Bible in one year.

☐ I will participate in a group Bible study through my church.

☐ I will spend at least five minutes each day before I leave my house praying for God to change _____ in my life, or for God to reveal blind spots in my life.

☐ Husbands: I will pray with my wife each day.

☐ I will pray with my children regularly (besides at mealtimes). For example, I may pray with my children before they leave for school each morning.

Let's talk! We will discuss:

☐ Any fresh spiritual decisions we might have made this weekend

☐ How our relationship with God affects our relationship with each other

☐ How we can encourage each other to have a stronger relationship with God

☐ Which side of the diagram on page 88 we're on

Let's learn! We will read the following book together:

☐ *Right With God* by John Blanchard

☐ *His Intimate Presence* by Bill Bright

☐ *First Love* by Bill Bright

☐ *More Than a Carpenter* by Josh McDowell

☐ *Spiritual Disciplines for the Christian Life* by Donald S. Whitney

☐ *The Discipline of Grace: God's Role and Our Role in the Pursuit of Holiness* by Jerry Bridges

6

7

Understanding: Communication I

Understanding: Communication 1

Session 7 Overview

Genuine communication requires
that a couple seeks to understand and to be understood.

I. The Anatomy of Understanding

[handwritten: language we use doesn't make sense (church bulletin) car insurance co)]

A. The couple who seeks to understand each other will __Value__ what it takes for genuine communication to occur.

1. Time

There is an appointed time for everything. And there is a time for every event under heaven ... A time to be silent, and a time to speak.

Ecclesiastes 3:1, 7b

2. Trust

There is no fear in love; but perfect love casts out fear, because fear involves punishment, and the one who fears is not perfected in love.

1 John 4:18

3. Transparency: sharing complete emotional and personal truthfulness. *[handwritten: sincere frank authentic]*

And the man and his wife were both naked and were not ashamed.

Genesis 2:25

B. Understanding increases with increased levels of communication.

COMMUNICATION LEVELS:	MEANING:	DEGREE OF TRANSPARENCY:	NUMBER OF PEOPLE:	
1. **Cliché**	Non-sharing			
2. **Fact**	Sharing what you know			**Degree of:** ◆ Trust ◆ Commitment ◆ Friendship
3. **Opinion**	Sharing what you think			
4. **Emotion**	Sharing what you feel			
5. **Transparency**	Sharing who you are			

(from, *Why Am I Afraid to Tell You Who I Am*, by John Powell)

((Roger & Elaine))

II. Listening: Seeking to Understand

But let everyone be quick to hear, slow to speak and slow to anger.

James 1:19b

No one cares how much you know until they know how much you care.

A. Many people want nothing more than someone to ___care___ enough to listen to them.

B. A poor listener will manifest habits that stifle communication and stir misunderstanding.

for men: Tell me more about it (don't try to fix it)

for women: shh, I'm watching the game

1. Pseudo-listening ___fakes___ interest.

2. Selective listening tunes in only for points of interest.

7

3. Protective listening doesn't hear any ___*threats*___ messages. *tune it out*

C. A good listener will manifest an ___*attitude*___ that encourages communication.

> *Be devoted to one another in brotherly love; give preference to one another in honor.*
>
> Romans 12:10

1. Listen with the attitude that your spouse's comments are top ___*priority*___; give focused attention. *don't treat them as an interruption of the day*

2. Listen with an attitude of ___*acceptance*___ and willingness to understand. *(body language—tone of voice)*

3. Listen with an attitude that your spouse is not your ___*enemy*___.

4. Listen with an attitude of willingness to hear what ___*God*___ may be saying through your spouse.

5. Listen with an attitude of wanting clarification. Ask questions and paraphrase in order to get at the meaning of the message.

7

Clarifying Questions	"Are you telling me that _____ ?"
	"What did you mean when you said _____ ?"
Commitment	"Of all that you just said, what do you most want me to understand?"
	"What do you need from me most right now?"

D. A good listener manifests proper listening habits that enhance communication.

FOCUS ON:	What is being said	The meaning	Clarification of valid points	Questions	Understanding
RATHER THAN:	The way it is being said	The words	Defense of incorrect accusations	Indictments	Judgment

Help me to understand what you just told me

E. Remember: Listening encourages understanding and builds oneness.

III. Expressing: Seeking to Be Understood

Sleepless in Seattle

A. People bring into marriage varying patterns of expressiveness.

we have diff styles

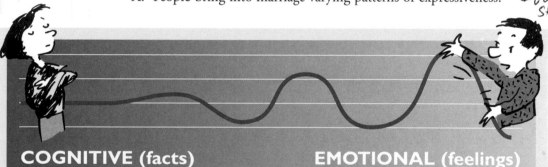

COGNITIVE (facts)
Closed, has difficulty expressing emotion

EMOTIONAL (feelings)
Open, has difficulty confining emotions

7

1. Misunderstanding can develop when two people are at opposite ends of the continuum.

2. A couple must allow ____freedom____ for differences in styles of expressiveness.

B. A variety of barriers keeps some from being understood.

be a man—
don't cry
be seen, not
heard

1. Childhood programming has established a ___pattern___ of suppression and repression in emotions.

2. A poor ___self image___ can cause one to fear rejection.

3. A false concept of manhood and ___pride___ prevents men from sharing their needs and feelings.

4. A false concept of spirituality makes us ___hesitant___ to share ourselves.

5. An ___angry___ heart sabotages understanding (James 1:19b, " ... be slow to anger").

C. Expressing ourselves involves the ___risk___ of being emotionally intimate.

1. Emotional intimacy involves expressing your feelings and emotions with someone who is committed to you.

   a. It begins by entrusting yourself to ___God___, because He understands.

   "Come to Me, all who are weary and heavy-laden, and I will give you rest."

   Matthew 11:28

   b. It follows by opening yourself to your ___spouse___, for his/understanding.
   her

   For this cause a man shall leave his father and his mother, and shall cleave to his wife and they shall become one flesh.

   Genesis 2:24

2. Emotional intimacy involves the disclosure of:

   • Thoughts

   • Feelings

   • Needs

D. Three steps toward expressing yourself:

Determine WHAT you want to say	Determine HOW you want to say it	Determine WHEN you want to say it
• What are my assumptions? • What are my beliefs? • What are my desires? • What are my dreams? • What are my needs?	• With excitement? • With sadness? • With conviction? • With disappointment? • With encouragement?	• During or after a meal? • During recreation? • At bedtime? • In the presence of children? • While driving?

IV. Summary

A. Developing understanding in marriage requires listening and expressing.

B. Will you make a commitment to:

1. Listen with understanding?

2. Express your thoughts, feelings, and needs?

3. Realize communication is a life-long process?

C. Remember, God's power is available to you when you are risking vulnerability with another person. *let go and let God*

D. Understanding grows in community. You will grow closer as a couple as you interact with other couples about how to build a stronger marriage.

Homebuilders

Take It Home

INDIVIDUAL APPLICATION

 I will do this! Check one or more of the following:

☐ This week, when my spouse is speaking, I will stop what I am doing, be fully attentive, and listen with a sincere attempt to understand before expressing my viewpoint.

☐ I will review the five levels of communication (page 93) and determine what steps we can take to move to the next level.

☐ I will make a date with my spouse sometime in the next 30 days to discuss the following questions:

    ☐ What could I do to make you feel more loved?

    ☐ What attribute would you like me to develop?

    ☐ What attribute would you like me to help you develop?

    ☐ What mutual goal would you like to see us accomplish?

    ☐ What could I do to make you feel more confident in our future direction?

☐ Sometime in the next 30 days, I will write a second love letter, reaffirming my appreciation, affection, and respect for my spouse (and I'll do it without expecting a letter in return!).

COUPLE APPLICATION

 Let's talk! We will discuss:

☐ What we can do to express ourselves more clearly or to be better listeners

☐ When we could communicate more effectively about important issues (the best time and best day)

☐ Starting a HomeBuilders group with friends from work, from our neighborhood, or from church

☐ Attending the alumni session at the Weekend to Remember Conference next year

Let's learn! We will read the following book together:

☐ *Communication—The Key to Your Marriage* by H. Norman Wright

☐ *The New Building Your Mate's Self-Esteem* by Dennis and Barbara Rainey

☐ *Improving Communication in Your Marriage* by Gary and Barbara Rosberg (part of the HomeBuilders Couples Series)

☐ *The Five Love Languages* by Gary Chapman

7

Strengthen Communication in Your Marriage Through a HomeBuilders Couples Series® Study Group

Application Project

Many of you may wonder, "How can we enhance oneness in our marriage once the conference is over?"

Oneness is strengthened when we follow some simple steps.

Steps to Enhancing Oneness

A. Study _____ _____ together on a regular basis.

B. Develop _____ with other couples.

C. Schedule consistent _____ to talk with your spouse about issues in your marriage and family.

D. Share _____ for achieving oneness with other couples.

The HomeBuilders Couples Series® provides a wonderful opportunity to build oneness in marriage!

HomeBuilders Overview

The Benefits of the HomeBuilders Couples Series

1. Spurs conversation between husband and wife.

2. Doesn't require an "expert" Bible teacher, just a facilitator.

3. Requires a short-term commitment.

4. Requires no preparation for the actual study.

5. Emphasizes practical application by completing the HomeBuilders Project.

6. Versatile in various situations: small groups, Sunday school classes, neighborhood outreaches, and weekend retreats.

7. Provides mutual encouragement and accountability.

8. Offers a diverse selection of topics to choose from.

9. Encourages further opportunities for marriage enrichment through FamilyLife Conferences and other resources.

10. Teaches more about how to live the Christian life.

11. Follows the biblical model of small groups (Matthew 28:18-20; Luke 6:12-16; Acts 2:42, 46-47).

HomeBuilders "Nuts and Bolts"

HomeBuilders Sessions follow the format below:

- **Focus**—A statement of the core studies for each session; read as session begins.

- **Warm Up**—A time for group members to get acquainted with one another, review the previous session, and begin new study. Have fun here, but don't prolong this segment.

- **Blueprints**—Biblical content; most of the time will be spent in this section.

- **HomeBuilders Principles**—Summary of points made throughout the study; points summary is to be emphasized.

- **Wrap Up**—This category serves to "bring home the point" and wind down a session in an appropriate fashion.

- **Make a Date**—Time for each couple to determine when to complete the HomeBuilders Project.

- **HomeBuilders Project**—60-90 minute timeframe for each couple to complete privately before the beginning of the next session.

- **Recommended Reading**—Suggestions for use of various resources to obtain maximum benefit from the study.

HomeBuilders Tips

1. Your Role as a "Facilitator" is to encourage others in the group to think and discover what Scripture says, help the group members feel comfortable and keep things moving forward. The facilitator is to provide an open, warm environment where couples accept one another. Facilitators will also want to review the Leader's Notes before each session.

2. The Ground Rules for HomeBuilders group members:
   - Share nothing that will embarrass your spouse.
   - You may pass on any question.
   - Complete the project with your spouse prior to each session.
   - Confidentiality—anything shared stays in the group

3. It is important to begin the group and end the sessions on time. Also, it is important for couples to make a commitment to attend all the sessions and complete each of the HomeBuilders projects.

Now for your marital enjoyment ...

A sample HomeBuilders study is printed on the following pages for use with this session. For further study as a couple or in a group, order copies of *Keeping Your Covenant*, a reproducible booklet that includes a sampling of four different HomeBuilders studies. This resource is available at no cost through FamilyLife's Web site: http://www.familylife.com/homebuilders /studies/sample.asp.

7

To Be Your Husband/Wife:
Making Your
Relationship a Priority

To develop positive communication patterns, you must make your
marriage relationship a priority.

W A R M • U P   15 M I N U T E S

"What I Like, How About You?"

In each of the following six categories, how do you see yourself? How do you see
your spouse? How does your spouse see you? On the spectrum for each category,
place a *Y* where you see yourself and an *S* where you see your spouse. When
you're finished, compare your results with your spouse's! Then share with the
group the one category in which your ratings most closely agreed or disagreed.

- **MUSIC**
  A little bit   Y ————————— S ————————————— A little bit
  country   rock 'n' roll

- **MOVIES**
  Comedy ——————————————————————————————— Drama

- **NUTRITION**
  Health food ————————————————————————— Junk food

- **FINANCES**
  "You can't take ——————————————— "A penny saved is
  it with you."   a penny earned."

- **VACATION**
  Go, go, go   Y ——————————— S ——— Slow down, relax

- **TECHNOLOGY**
  Wired ——————————————————————————————— Off-line

7

A relationship is a living thing—it thrives with attention and withers when ignored. To maintain a healthy relationship, married couples should regularly examine how they spend their most precious resources—their time and energy—and determine whether they are following their priorities. Many couples find that each anniversary is a good time to evaluate priorities together.

Your Most Precious Resources

1. What pressures in your life make it a challenge for you to give your marriage the time and energy it needs to grow stronger?

children

2. How do the following passages relate to making your marriage and home a priority in your lives?

Ephesians 5:15-16

Therefore be careful how you walk, not as unwise men but as wise, making the most of your time, because the days are evil.

TV, comp electronics

Philippians 2:1-4

Therefore if there is any encouragement in Christ, if there is any consolation of love, if there is any fellowship of the Spirit, if any affection and compassion, make my joy complete by being of the same mind, maintaining the same love, united in spirit, intent on one purpose. Do nothing from selfishness or empty conceit, but with humility of mind regard one another as more important than yourselves; do not merely look out for your own personal interests, but also for the interests of others.

Song of Solomon 7:10-13

"I am my beloved's, and his desire is for me. "Come, my beloved, Let us go out into the country, Let us spend the night in the villages, "Let us rise early and go to the vineyards; Let us see whether the vine has budded And its blossoms have opened, And whether the pomegranates have bloomed. There I will give you my love. The mandrakes have given forth fragrance; And over our doors are all choice fruits, Both new and old, Which I have saved up for you, my beloved.

take time for each other

3. What good examples of making a marriage relationship a priority have you seen modeled by other couples?

4. What effect would you say that priority has had on those couples' marriages?

5. What are some things you've done lately to make your relationship a priority?

Personalizing Your Marriage Priorities

Answer questions 6, 7, and 8 with your spouse. After answering, you may want to share an appropriate insight or discovery with the group.

6. How are you doing in making your marriage a priority?

7. What are some of the barriers you face as you think of taking time for your spouse every day?

8. As you look at your normal daily schedule, what could you change—what could you spend less time doing—to make more room for your relationship? What would be the best time of the day for you to set aside for time together?

Recreational Companionship

9. What have been some fun, creative dates you've had together since you were married? What type of effect have these had on your relationship?

10. What would it take for you to go out on dates—or on weekends together, away from the kids—more than you do?

Conserving Your Energy

11. What would happen if you were able to transfer the energy you normally give to your work to your family instead? What would that do to your family? What would that do to your work?

12. Understanding that transferring all of your energy from work to your family is likely impossible, what are some ways you *could* save more energy for your home life?

7

HomeBuilders Principle:
For communication within a marriage to be effective, you must reserve time and energy for your spouse.

Wishing-Not Well

Dig out five coins. Any coins will do—but you may be permanently giving up these coins. Form a circle if you aren't already in one. Close your eyes, and listen as the leader reads the following questions. Don't answer verbally, but for every question that you must answer "yes," toss one coin into the center of the circle. Try not to notice how others around you are responding.

- Within the last month, have you ever let your day get so full that you barely had time to say good morning and good night to your spouse?

- Have you recently ignored your spouse—even for a minute—because of something your were watching on television?

- Within the last year, have you let work obliterate a time together that the two of you had planned in advance?

- Within the last six months, have you let a dispute over children, friends, or activities come between you?

- Have you ever let a hobby or other interest consume so much of your time that your spouse felt neglected?

Now open your eyes and look at all the coins in the center of your circle. Silently think about how each coin represents at least one dent in someone's marriage relationship. Consider what commitment you might want to make to God regarding making your marriage more of a priority in your life. If you feel comfortable doing so, share with the group any commitment you want to make. Then gather all the coins together and have someone buy a treat (however small) for your next meeting.

Make a Date

Make a date with your spouse to meet before the next session to complete the HomeBuilders Project. Your leader will ask you to share one thing from this experience.

DATE

TIME

LOCATION

As a Couple (10 minutes)

- Begin by sharing at least one example of a time you thought your spouse really made your marriage a priority.

- Tell your spouse about any commitment you made or considered making during the last session.

Individually (25 minutes)

1. What insight about communication in marriage have you gained from this session?

2. How do you feel about the amount of time and energy you are saving each day for your spouse? for your children?

3. How do you feel about the amount of time and energy your spouse saves each day for you? for your children?

7

4. What difference do you think receiving more of your spouse's time and energy would make in your life?

5. What could you do to make your marriage and your family a higher priority in your life? What will you do this week?

6. What differences do you think a change in priorities would make in your relationship and communication with your spouse?

Interact as a Couple (25 minutes)

1. Share your answers from previous questions.

2. If you haven't already chosen a time, what would be a good time each day for you to spend talking together? You might want to start with just ten minutes, but set a time and stick with it.

3. What changes would you need to make—and what obstacles would you need to overcome—to spend this time together?

4. Pray together, committing to God to follow through on making your marriage a higher priority this week.

Remember to take your calendar to the next session so you can Make a Date.

Commonly Asked Questions about the HomeBuilders Couples Series

1. What is the best size group?

We recommend from four to seven couples (including you and your spouse). If you have more people interested than you think you can accommodate, consider having someone else lead a second group.

2. Should an individual join the group alone?

It is best if a person does not join HomeBuilders alone. Learning the principles and seeing everyone else working together on their marriages would cause discouragement and dissatisfaction with the individual's spouse. This does not mean if a person's spouse is out of town, perhaps on business, that the couple should skip the study. If one spouse is a regular member, the other should attend.

3. What time schedule should we follow?

The material presented in each session is designed for a 90-minute study; however, we recommend a two-hour block of time. This will allow you to move through each part of the study at a more relaxed pace, and include time for fellowship or refreshments. However, be sure to keep in mind one of the cardinal rules of a small group: Good groups start and end on time. People's time is valuable, and your group will appreciate your being respectful of this.

4. What is the group leader's responsibility?

It is critical that you assume the role of facilitator. Help the group interact and discuss the information. Be careful not to lecture or allow the group to ramble aimlessly. Guide the group using the leader's tips and notes at the back of this booklet. Strongly encourage group members to complete every project — by doing so they will get the most from the sessions. Commit to pray regularly for the couples in your group.

Next Steps

HomeBuilders is easy and fun! It is simple to get started.

1. Obtain copies of the *Keeping your Covenant* study by:
   a. Downloading for free at http://www.familylife.com/homebuilders/studies/sample.asp
   b. Making your purchase in the Weekend to Remember Resource Center.
   c. Calling 1-800-FL-TODAY (358-6329), 24 hours a day.

2. Select a time and date to begin the study. Then decide how often to meet.

3. Invite friends, church members, or neighbors to your home (about four couples is a comfortable number).

4. Pray for your group!

That's all there is to it! Invest in relationships today—yours and others.

7

HomeBuilders Couples Series®

Check out these HomeBuilders Couples Series studies at the
Weekend to Remember Resource Center!

Building Your Marriage*

Building Your Mate's Self-Esteem

Building Teamwork in Your Marriage

*Improving Communication
in Your Marriage**

Resolving Conflict in Your Marriage

Mastering Money in Your Marriage

Growing Together in Christ

Overcoming Stress in Your Marriage

Making Your Remarriage Last

Defending the Military Marriage

HomeBuilders Leader's Guide

Keeping Your Covenant*

*Available in Spanish

HomeBuilders Parenting Series®

Improving Your Parenting

Guiding Your Teenagers

Raising Children of Faith

Building Character in Your Children

*Establishing Effective Discipline
for Your Children*

Helping Your Children Know God

You can order HomeBuilders studies by calling **1-800-FL-TODAY**
(358-6329), 24 hours a day, or by visiting **www.familylife.com**. Register to
become a part of the **HomeBuilders Leadership Network** at our Web site to
be equipped, educated, and encouraged as a HomeBuilders group facilitator.

Sexual Intimacy: Communication II

8

Sexual Intimacy: Communication II

 Session 8 Overview

A satisfying sex life is the result of a satisfying relationship.

I. All of us have differing ideas, expectations, and standards about sex.

Let the cat out

A. Sex is ___God's___ idea.

 And God created man in His own image, in the image of God He created him; male and female He created them ... For this cause a man shall leave his father and his mother, and shall cleave to his wife; and they shall become one flesh.

Genesis 1:27 and 2:24

B. Sex is the divine ___process___ of implementing God's command to multiply a godly legacy.

 And God blessed them; and God said to them, "Be fruitful and multiply, and fill the earth, and subdue it; and rule over the fish of the sea and over the birds of the sky, and over every living thing that moves on the earth."

Genesis 1:28

C. Sex was created to be experienced only in the context of marriage (1 Corinthians 7:1-2).

D. Sex is a gift from God and designed for our _____pleasure_____.

THE HUSBAND HAS THE FREEDOM TO ENJOY HIS WIFE'S BODY	THE WIFE HAS THE FREEDOM TO ENJOY HER HUSBAND'S BODY
How beautiful are your feet in sandals, O prince's daughter! The curves of your hips are like jewels, the work of the hands of an artist. Your navel is like a round goblet which never lacks mixed wine; your belly is like a heap of wheat fenced about with lilies. Your two breasts are like two fawns, twins of a gazelle. Your neck is like a tower of ivory, your eyes like the pools in Heshbon by the gate of Bath-rabbim; your nose is like the tower of Lebanon, which faces toward Damascus. Your head crowns you like Carmel, and the flowing locks of your head are like purple threads; the king is captivated by your tresses. How beautiful and how delightful you are, my love, with all your charms! Your stature is like a palm tree, and your breasts are like its clusters. I said, 'I will climb the palm tree, I will take hold of its fruit stalks.' Oh, may your breasts be like clusters of the vine, and the fragrance of your breath like apples, and your mouth like the best wine! It goes down smoothly for my beloved, flowing gently through the lips of those who fall asleep.	*My beloved is dazzling and ruddy, outstanding among ten thousand. His head is like gold, pure gold; his locks are like clusters of dates, and black as a raven. His eyes are like doves, beside streams of water, bathed in milk, and reposed in their setting. His cheeks are like a bed of balsam, banks of sweet-scented herbs; his lips are lilies, dripping with liquid myrrh. His hands are rods of gold set with beryl; his abdomen is carved ivory inlaid with sapphires. His legs are pillars of alabaster set on pedestals of pure gold; his appearance is like Lebanon, choice as the cedars. His mouth is full of sweetness. and he is wholly desirable. This is my beloved and this is my friend, O daughters of Jerusalem.*
Song of Solomon 7:1-9	Song of Solomon 5:10-16

physical   character

8

II. A satisfying sex life is the result of a satisfying marriage relationship.

A. A satisfying marriage relationship grows best when a couple places value on:

1. Creating _Companionship_ .

This is my beloved and this is my friend, O daughters of Jerusalem.

Song of Solomon 5:16b

2. Strengthening _Commitment_ .

Put me like a seal over your heart, like a seal on your arm. For love is as strong as death ...

Song of Solomon 8:6a

3. Encouraging _passion_ .

You have made my heart beat faster, my sister, my bride; you have made my heart beat faster with a single glance of your eyes, with a single strand of your necklace.

Song of Solomon 4:9

... My feelings were aroused for him.

Song of Solomon 5:4b

4. Growing in _spiritual intimacy_ .

B. Companionship, commitment, passion, and spiritual intimacy combine to create an environment where the sexual relationship can flourish.

8

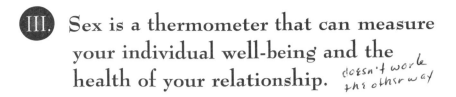

III. **Sex is a thermometer that can measure your individual well-being and the health of your relationship.** *doesn't work the other way*

A. Because sex is a physical, mental, emotional, and spiritual activity, it can reflect your individual well-being in any of these areas.

1. Sex can reflect your ___*physical*___ condition.

   - Fatigue
   - Diet
   - Exercise
   - Pregnancy
   - Dysfunction *10% physical 90% emotional*

2. Sex can reflect your ___*mental*___ well-being.

   - Stress
   - Preoccupation
   - Incorrect information *about sex* *learned from / peers / media*
   1% church 3% dad 12% mom 7% school *68%*

3. Sex can reflect your ___*emotional*___ health.

   - Abuse: verbal, physical, emotional, sexual
     4) guard your tongue
   - Anger: Displaced, chronic, and unresolved conflict
   - Guilt: real or false
   - Self-worth *(caress w/ words)*

4. Sex can reflect your ___*spiritual*___ condition.

   - Unconfessed sin
   - Spiritual dryness
   - Unreconciled relationships

Have to separate fantasy from reality

Lust (more) Love (satisfied)

B. If the marriage relationship is lacking in companionship, commitment, passion, or spiritual intimacy, the sexual relationship may register the problem.

1. When *companionship* is lacking, sex often loses its
   _____depth_____ .

2. When *commitment* is lacking, sex can seem _____risky_____ and vulnerable.

3. When *passion* is lacking, sex can become _____routine_____ .

4. When *spiritual intimacy* is lacking, sex can become _____shallow_____ and self-focused.

brain & heart & mouth

IV. Sex in marriage can be improved by understanding differences.

A. Differences between men and women

	MEN		WOMEN	
am I able to please women	Physical	**Attitude**	Relational	*Care we r really friends*
argue? settle	Compartmentalized		Wholistic	
show love sex			*sex begins at breakfast - all day deal*	
physical	Body-centered	**Stimulation**	Person-centered	*caress, cuddle, talk*
	Sight		Touch (foreplay)	
	Fragrance		Attitudes	
	Actions		Words (truth)	
	Respect	**Needs**	Security	
	To be physically needed		To be emotionally needed	
	Physical expression		Intimacy	
AAA anytime, anywhere, anytime *no cycle*	Acyclical	**Sexual Response** *micro wave*	Cyclical	
	Quick excitement		Slower excitement *crock pot*	
	Difficult to distract		Easily distracted	
	Shorter, more intense	**Orgasm**	Longer, more in-depth	
	More physically oriented		More emotionally oriented	

B. Differences between perspectives

WHEN YOU FOCUS ON ...	YOUR ATTITUDE TOWARD SEX TENDS TO ...
Companionship	be tender and pleasurable be an expression of the overall relationship begin with conversation and time together
Commitment	be deep and meaningful be the most profound experience of life be a very serious thing
Passion	be fun be explosive and impetuous be playful and passionate
Spiritual Intimacy	be holy and reverent be selfless and sacrificial be seen as one of God's good gifts

C. When we learn to accept and enjoy the differences we have in the marriage relationship, the sexual relationship will flourish.

V. Sex in marriage can be improved by building and balancing companionship, commitment, passion, and spiritual intimacy.

A. Companionship is cultivated through romance, tenderness, and communication.

1. Romance

    a. Share mutual interest (walks, ~~biking~~ home improvement)

    b. Revive the lost art of dating

2. Tenderness

    a. Give creative expressions of affection

    b. Show your love through non-sexual touch

3. Communication

8

B. Commitment is forged through faithfulness, respect, and forgiveness.

  1. Faithfulness

     a. Build or rebuild trust.

     b. Develop a healthy attitude toward your partner.

     c. Develop a healthy attitude toward sex.

  2. Forgiveness

C. Passion is fired through planning, unselfishness (or generosity), and creativity.

  1. Plan

     a. Make it a priority.

     b. Schedule it in the best part of your day.

  2. Be unselfish.

     a. Commit to a mutually fulfilling sex life.

     pleasing spouse most important

        Let the husband fulfill his duty to his wife, and likewise also the wife to her husband. The wife does not have authority over her own body, but the husband does; and likewise also the husband does not have authority over his own body, but the wife does.

        1 Corinthians 7:3-4

  3. Be creative

     a. Enhance the setting. *backrubs - women food - men*

     b. Vary the approach.

D. Spiritual intimacy is cultivated through prayer, truth, and love.

  1. Pray together.

  2. Spend time together in God's Word.

VI. Summary

A. Sex is not an end; it is the means to an end.

B. The end we seek is a marriage relationship filled with companionship, commitment, passion, and spiritual intimacy.

C. Remember: A satisfying sex life is the result of a satisfying marriage relationship.

8

Sexual Intimacy: Expression of Oneness

Application Project

This application project has two sections: the individual section and the interaction section. Be sure to leave adequate time to interact as a couple on the interaction section.

Individual Section

25 Minutes

Setting: Stay together as a couple, but complete this section quickly without any interaction.

Objective: To open up communication by surfacing and identifying personal feelings, attitudes, and thoughts you have on this subject.

Instructions: Complete this section individually.

Part One:

How satisfied are you with the way you and your spouse handle the following aspects of your sexual relationship? Circle the number that corresponds to your answer. Underline the answer you think your spouse will select.

LOW SATISFACTION					HIGH SATISFACTION	
1	2	3	4	5		The quality of our companionship.
1	2	3	4	5		The level of our commitment.
1	2	3	4	5		The fire of our passion.
1	2	3	4	5		The depth of our spiritual intimacy
1	2	3	4	5		Viewing sex with positive anticipation.
1	2	3	4	5		The way we decide to have sex together.
1	2	3	4	5		The amount of communication during lovemaking (such as discussing better ways of pleasing each other).
1	2	3	4	5		The frequency of our physical intimacy.
1	2	3	4	5		Gentleness and tenderness during lovemaking.
1	2	3	4	5		The variety of our sexual experiences together.
1	2	3	4	5		The selflessness displayed in our lovemaking.
1	2	3	4	5		The understanding I have of my spouse in this area.
1	2	3	4	5		The overall temperature of our love for one another.

8

Part Two:

Answer the following questions.

1. List any fears you may have about sex. How can your spouse alleviate these fears? How can a deeper realization of God's love help?

2. Do you fully trust your spouse with your body? If not, in what aspect? Why? Refer to 1 Corinthians 7:3-5.

3. List any incorrect attitudes you may have about your body or your spouse's body. Refer to Song of Solomon 5:1-16 and 7:1-9.

Part Three:

Complete the following:

1. In leading up to physical love, I like for you to ...

2. When we are sharing physical love, I like for you to ...

8

3. I feel discouraged when you ...

4. I am most drawn to you sexually when you ...

Part Four:

1. Look back over parts one through three and note what changes in your own behavior could make improvements in your physical relationship.

2. In prayer, confess any resentment and bitterness you may have.

3. Recognize that sex is a gift from God and that an attitude of giving establishes oneness.

4. Agree together that your sexual union is a reflection of your intimacy and union with one another and with God in Jesus Christ.

8

Interaction Section

30 Minutes

Setting: Stay together as a couple and complete this section.

Objective: To discuss the feelings, attitudes, and thoughts that each of you have on this subject.

Instructions:

1. Share and discuss as a couple the work you completed in parts one through four. Be sure to interact with an attitude of understanding, sympathy, and forgiveness.

2. Schedule a whole day and night within the next month when both of you can get away for a special time of communication and intimacy.

3. Pray together and thank God for each other as His provision. Make a commitment to each other to improve communication and intimacy.

4. Write the points of action you will take individually, as a couple, and with others on the *Take It Home* page.

5. Then, record that point of action you most want to apply on the *Take It Home Summary* flap attached to the back cover.

8

Take It Home

| INDIVIDUAL APPLICATION | COUPLE APPLICATION |

 I will do this! Check one or more of the following:

☐ In order to forge a stronger bond with my spouse, I will never weaken the foundation of our relationship by threatening or suggesting the possibility of divorce. I will ask my spouse to forgive me if I have made those kinds of threats in the past.

☐ To cultivate a healthier romantic relationship, I want to plan some kind of fun, creative, and romantic time together with my spouse once a month (see the FamilyLife Resource Center for creative help in this area).

☐ Recognizing how different we are as men and women in this area, I will work to be more understanding and more sympathetic to my spouse's desires and needs for intimacy.

☐ I will seek to say positive and affirming things about my spouse's appearance, instead of saying hurtful or negative things.

☐ I need to buy a new nightgown or some pajamas!

☐ If we aren't able to complete our project during this weekend (the one we're supposed to do tonight), we will schedule a time in the next 30 days to finish it.

☐ I will learn to be less demanding and more sensitive to my spouse's intimacy needs.

 Let's talk! We will discuss:

☐ Fun, non-sexual things we can do together to help recapture the companionship we experienced when we were dating

☐ The chart on page 116 that outlines the differences between men and women in this area, and what's true or not true about us

☐ My struggle with pornography or with romantic fantasies, and how we can work together to experience freedom from these traps

☐ The impact my past history of sexual activity (including past sexual abuse) may have had on our sexual relationship

 Let's learn! We will read the following book together:

☐ *Simply Romantic® Nights* from FamilyLife

☐ *Sexual Intimacy in Marriage* by William Cutrer and Sandra Glahn

☐ *Love Life for Every Married Couple* by Ed Wheat

☐ *Intimate Issues* by Linda Dillow and Lorraine Pintus (for women who want more insight into the sexual dimensions of marriage)

☐ *The Wounded Heart* by Dan Allender (especially for those with a past history of sexual abuse)

☐ *Reclaiming Intimacy* by Heather Jamison (for those who may have been sexually active prior to marriage)

☐ *Every Man's Battle* by Fred Stoeker and Stephen Arterburn (for men who are committed to moral purity in their marriage)

8

Engagement:
Preparation for
Oneness

Engagement: Preparation for Oneness

Session 9 Overview

Practical suggestions for beginning your life together as one.

I. The first year of marriage will require a surprising number of adjustments.

A. Sharing your personal space

B. Adjusting to each other's personal habits

C. Making decisions as a team that you once made alone

II. The first year of marriage may seem harder than you thought it would be.

A. You may discover an unexpected number of differences between you.

   1. Male/female differences

   2. Different personalities and temperaments

   3. Different styles of communication

B. You may be surprised by the impact of your spouse's past or family.

    1. You may have different expectations about roles.

    2. You will have to begin to adjust to your spouse's family.

    3. You or your spouse may have brought more baggage from the past than you thought.

C. You can begin to prepare now for your first year of marriage.

    1. You can discuss anticipated adjustments in advance.

    2. You can examine your expectations for the first year of marriage.

III. Beginning a sexual relationship requires wisdom and sensitivity.

A. Understanding and dealing with your sexual past

    1. Understanding how you think about sex

        a. Movies, books, and magazines may have affected your expectations about sex.

        b. Past sexual relationships may cause you to make hurtful comparisons.

    2. What is appropriate to share with your spouse about your sexual past?

B. Beginning your sexual relationship in marriage

    1. Sexual differences between men and women

        a. Anatomy and stimulation

        b. Myths about sex

        c. Wisdom regarding the wedding night

C. Preparing now for your future together

   1. Learn how to grow together spiritually

      a. Pray together

      b. Read God's Word together

      c. Serve God together

   2. Develop habits to continue cultivating companionship

      a. Don't stop dating

      b. Learn each other's love language

   3. Be ready for the common "danger zones" during the first years of marriage

      a. Adjusting to living together

      b. Expectations of each other

      c. Finances

      d. Conflict resolution

      e. Sex

      f. Children

      g. Stress

   4. Know where to go for help

      a. Your church

      b. A mentor couple

      c. Books, tapes, other resources

The following outline is additional information to session five to help both men and women discern the will of God.

Five practical steps for affirming your commitment to marriage

1. **Get alone with God.**

    a. Make this a regular habit.

    b. Spend time reading God's Word and in prayer.

2. **Make sure you are right with God. Confess your sins and humble yourself before Him. Relinquish all rights to your life to God.**

     If I regard wickedness in my heart, the Lord will not hear.
    Psalm 66:18

3. **If you are troubled by doubts, write them down in a list.**

    a. Honestly evaluate each one by asking yourself:

        1) Is this fear the result of legitimate questions in my mind?

        2) Does it merely demonstrate a lack of trust in God's direction?

    b. Discuss your doubts and concerns with your partner. Then ask yourself:

        1) Did my partner receive or resist my concerns?

        2) Is my partner open to correcting these relationship problems?

        3) Is my partner willing and able to give and ask for forgiveness?

4. **If you decide that it is not God's will for you to marry:**

   a. It is essential that you make a clean break. (Remember, a broken relationship is better than a broken marriage!)

   b. We strongly suggest that there be no communication for six months.

   c. If, after that time, you think God may be leading you back together, you should seek wise counsel before re-establishing contact.

5. **If you decide that it is God's will for you to marry:**

   a. Ask Him to confirm His will during the upcoming weeks or months. God probably won't give you a visible or audible "sign," but His Spirit can give you an inner confidence that you are headed in the right direction.

   b. Be honest with yourself, obedient to God, and open to do what is right in the sight of your partner.

Remember: God's will is ultimately known by faith!

 And without faith it is impossible to please Him, for he who comes to God must believe that He is and that He is a rewarder of those who seek Him.

Hebrews 11:6

The Wife's Responsibility for Oneness

The Wife's Responsibility for Oneness

Session 10 Overview

The fulfillment of a wife's role in marriage leads to oneness.

Can't △ our husbands – can only △ ourselves

I. Wife's responsibility: Accept God's design for marriage.

good judgement common sense

A. A wise woman walks with ___discernment___.

Sometimes we handle our marriage like a garage sale

> Therefore be careful how you walk, not as unwise men, but as wise, making the most of your time, because the days are evil.
>
> Ephesians 5:15-16

B. God has designed the husband and the wife with

___Equal___ ___value___.

> There is neither Jew nor Greek, there is neither slave nor free man, there is neither male nor female, for you are all one in Christ Jesus.
>
> Galatians 3:28

C. God has designed the husband and the wife to be

___interdependent___.

fill each other's gap like 2 spools of thread on a sewing machine

> However in the Lord, neither is woman independent of man, nor is man independent of woman.
>
> 1 Corinthians 11:11

D. A wise woman discerns God's divine order of responsibility in marriage.

1. God has designated the husband as the ___head___ of the relationship.

   b) leads & serves
   provider, protector

    For the husband is the head of the wife, as Christ is also the head of the church, He Himself being the Savior of the body.

   world has skewed meaning Ephesians 5:23
   of head (not boss, dictator...)

2. God has given the wife to the man as his ___helper___ in the relationship.

   Not a subordinate
   strong person that comes to aid of someone

    Then the Lord God said, "It is not good for the man to be alone; I will make him a helper suitable for him."

   Genesis 2:18

   a. "Helper" is a title of ___worth___. God refers to Himself in Scripture as our helper.

    Behold, God is my helper; the Lord is the sustainer of my soul.

   Psalm 54:4

   b. Jesus refers to the Holy Spirit as "another helper."

    And I will ask the Father, and He will give you another Helper, that He may be with you forever; that is the Spirit of truth,

   John 14:16-17a

3. God has designed the husband-wife relationship to be a living picture of the relationship between Christ and the church.

E. God has provided the husband and the wife the power to fulfill His design through dependence upon His Spirit.

    "For apart from Me, you can do nothing."

   John 15:5b

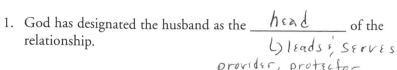

CHRIST

GLORIFY
SUBMIT

CHURCH

10

II. Wife's responsibility: Loving her husband

infatuation

cute as Robert Redford
funny as Woody Allen
smart as Albert Einstein

Love
cute as Woody Allen
funny as Albert Einstein
smart as Robert Redford
and it's ok

... encourage the young women to love their husbands.

Titus 2:4

A. Love is an attitude of unconditional acceptance.

1. Accept your husband as he is—an imperfect person. Your acceptance should not be based upon his performance, but on his _____worth_____ as God's gift to you.

2. Accept his thoughts and feelings.

Keep your eyes wide open before marriage and only 1/2 open afterwards.
Ben Franklin

3. Accept him despite his _____failures_____. True love grants another person the freedom to fail, allowing the Holy Spirit to work in another person's life.

(— agape commitment love)

B. Love is a sacrificial _____action_____.

best gift to kids is a marriage that loves one another

1. Love is keeping your husband in focus as your top _____priority_____.

(friendship love)

2. Love is staying available to your husband in terms of _____time_____ and energy.

↳ don't give all your time to kids

3. Love is listening.

C. Love is physical _____responsiveness_____.

physical love

knows what makes him tick what tickles him and what ticks him off

I am my beloved's and his desire is for me. Come, my beloved, let us go out into the country, let us spend the night in the villages. Let us rise early and go to the vineyards ... there I will give you my love.

Song of Solomon 7:10-12

10

III. Wife's responsibility: Supporting her husband

An excellent wife, who can find? For her worth is far above jewels. The heart of her husband trusts in her, and he will have no lack of gain. She does him good and not evil all the days of her life.

Proverbs 31:10-12

A. Support is a ___complimentary___, not competitive way of relating to your husband. (team)

It is better to live in a corner of a roof than in a house shared with a contentious woman.

Proverbs 21:9

B. Support will help your husband become a more godly man and sacrificial servant-leader.

pray for your husband

An excellent wife is the crown of her husband, but she who shames him is as rottenness to his bones.

Proverbs 12:4

1. He needs your support in his ___job___. *proud of what he does*

2. He needs your support in ___public___.

3. He needs your support in the ___home___. *little things that show*

constructive criticism good, but not in public

C. He needs your support as the leader of the relationship.

1. This support is called ___submission___ in Scripture.

Wives, submit to your own husbands, as to the Lord. For the husband is the head of the wife, as Christ is also is the head of the church ...

Ephesians 5:22-23 (ESV)

Note: When you submit to your husband, you model to him, your children, and the world the relationship of Christ's bride (the Church) to her Lord and Savior, Jesus Christ.

2. Submission does not mean:

  a. To be inferior

  b. To lose your identity and become a non-person

  c. Blind obedience

  d. You should feel used

  e. Allowing your husband to violate the law or to be physically abusive

  f. Following your husband into sin

3. Submission does mean:

  a. Responding to your husband's leadership with a view to God's design for marriage

  b. _____Encouraging_____ your husband to lead by willingly coming under his leadership

  give & take

  c. _____Assisting_____ your husband to lead by encouraging his initiative

  praying for husband

  Submission is not about logic, it is about love

  d. _____Praying_____ for your husband

  e. Honoring God's Word

  ... Being subject to their own husbands, that the Word of God might not be dishonored.

  Titus 2:5b

IV. Wife's responsibility: Respecting her husband

... and let the wife see to it that she respect her husband.

Ephesians 5:33b

... and let the wife see that she respects and reverences her husband—that she notices him, regards him, honors him, prefers him, venerates and esteems him; and that she defers to him, praises him, and loves and admires him exceedingly.

Ephesians 5:33b (Amplified Bible)

A. Respect means to ___voluntary___ regard another person with honor, esteem, and deference.

B. Respecting your husband involves ___understanding___ and ___appreciation___.

1. Understand and appreciate the weight of his responsibilities and pressures.

2. Understand and appreciate his unique needs as a man. *(HIS NEEDS / HER NEEDS)*

3. Understand and appreciate his differences as a man.

C. ___Encouragement___ demonstrates respect that gives confidence to your husband.

1. Encouragement means saying and doing things that build him up.

2. Encouragement says, "I believe in you."

D. _____Admiration_____ demonstrates respect that energizes your husband.

    1. Admiration praises a husband for the things he does _____right_____ .

    2. Admiration says, "I'm proud of you."

dwell on the good of your husband

V. Summary

10

A. Becoming a helper to your husband involves two basic responsibilities.

    1. It begins with an _____attitude_____ of entrusting yourself to God.

> *Therefore, let those also who suffer according to the will of God entrust their souls to a faithful Creator in doing what is right.*
>
> 1 Peter 4:19

    2. It requires a _____decision_____ of the will.

B. As you commit yourself to God's design for marriage, you will be able to demonstrate the love, support, and respect your husband needs to become the servant-leader God has called him to be.

C. Remember, God has designed a husband and wife to fulfill their roles and responsibilities through dependence upon His Spirit and His Word.

The following charts* will compare the bitter thoughts a wife might think about her husband with kind, tenderhearted, and forgiving thoughts based on God's Word.

Bitter Thoughts	Kind, Tenderhearted, and Forgiving Thoughts
He doesn't love me. He only loves himself.	*He does not show love as he should but his capacity to love can grow.* Colossians 3:14
How dare he come in from work in a bad mood and take it out on me!	*Perhaps he feels under pressure from work.* Ephesians 4:31-32
I do so much for him and look what I get in return!	*I wonder if I could do something differently to make it easier for him.* Philippians 2:3-4
He's only thinking of himself.	*Maybe he doesn't feel well today.* Colossians 3:12
He's stupid; see if I ever try to talk to him again!	*Maybe he misunderstood what I was trying to say.* Ephesians 4:1-3
I can't believe what he decided. How ridiculous!	*Maybe he has information that I don't have.* 1 Corinthians 4:5
I can't believe what he has done to me!	*What he has done is difficult, but God will give me the grace to get through it.* 1 Corinthians 10:13
I will never forgive him.	*After all that the Lord has forgiven me, this is the least that I can do.* Matthew 18:32-33
He'll never change.	*By God's grace, he can change.* 1 Corinthians 6:11
This is more than I can bear. There is no hope.	*There is <u>nothing</u> that has happened that God cannot forgive, that I cannot forgive, and that we can't work through.* 1 John 1:9
He did that on purpose to hurt me.	*Only God can know why he did what he did. It's my responsibility to believe the best.* 1 Corinthians 13:7

10

*Taken from *The Excellent Wife* by Martha Peace, (Focus Publishing, Bemidji, MN, 1995, 1999) pp 94-95. Used by permission.

Bitter Thoughts	Kind, Tenderhearted, and Forgiving Thoughts
We never should have gotten married in the first place.	He is my husband and I am <u>committed</u> to him no matter what. Matthew 19:6
God understands that I can't take this.	God will give me the wisdom and grace to hang in there. James 1:5
I prayed about it and have "peace" about pursuing the divorce.	It would be nice to have this settled but I am committed to proceeding in the way God has determined. Colossians 3:2
I wish he were dead.	I pray that God will have mercy on him and he will repent. 2 Peter 3:9
I hate him.	I can show love to him whether I feel like it or not. 1 Corinthians 13:4-7
He is repulsive to me. The thought of him touching me is nauseating.	My husband desiring to have sex with me is a good thing. I can show love to him by <u>concentrating</u> on pleasing him. 1 Corinthians 4:5
How could God let him do this to me?	God has a <u>purpose</u> in all that I am experiencing. He can and will use it for my good if I respond in love to God. Romans 8:28-29
I'll show him what it's like.	I'll give him a blessing instead. 1 Peter 3:9
He should have known better.	How could he possibly know? I've never told him. He can't read my mind. Ephesians 4:15

10

Take It Home

INDIVIDUAL APPLICATION	COUPLE APPLICATION

 I will do this! Check one or more of the following:

☐ I will look this week for specific ways I can support my husband and affirm his leadership in our relationship.

☐ I will work (in the power of the Holy Spirit) to guard my tongue and to avoid critical words or a complaining attitude.

☐ I will find an opportunity every day this week to show that I understand, appreciate, encourage and admire my husband.

☐ I will seek out a godly older woman who can be a model and a mentor for me in my relationship with my husband.

☐ I will look for ways to let my husband know that I respect and desire him sexually.

 Let's talk! We will discuss:

☐ Sometime in the next 30 days, I will ask my husband to answer the following four questions:

    ☐ What one thing could I do that would make it easier for you to be the leader in our home?

    ☐ What is one thing I can do to make our home a more inviting place for you?

    ☐ What goals do you have at work or for our family, and how can I help you achieve them?

    ☐ What would indicate to you that I really desire to be more Christ-like?

 Let's learn! I will read the following book:

☐ *The Excellent Wife* by Martha Peace

☐ *The Power of a Praying Wife* by Stormie Omartian

☐ *A Biblical Portrait of Womanhood* by Nancy Leigh DeMoss

☐ *Rocking The Roles* by Robert Lewis and William Hendricks

Session Eleven

II

Mom

You know your a mom when time to shave only one leg
count sprinkles on each kids cupcake to make sure they are equa

fast forward Bambi
use your spit to clean kids face

Mom

Session 11 Overview

The character of a mom has lasting influence on her children.

If it was going to be easy it wouldn't start with labor

I. God's perspective of motherhood

A. Mom has a ___lasting / powerful___ influence.

B. Mom is ___irreplacable___ in the family.

C. A woman's upbringing shapes her value of motherhood.

   1. How has your mother influenced your feelings and values concerning the family and children?

   2. What are your fears about being a mom?

D. Motherhood is not ___impossible___.

   1. Your view of motherhood does not have to be tainted by the deficiencies in your upbringing.

2. Motherhood is cultivated by:

   a. Seeking guidance from God's Word

   b. Being filled with the Holy Spirit

   c. Seeking an older woman as a role model (Titus 2:3-4)

   d. Becoming a mentor for a younger mom

   e. Reading helpful books

   f. Godly counsel

E. Motherhood is a high and holy __calling__.

> *Behold, children are a gift of the Lord; the fruit of the womb is a reward.*
>
> Psalm 127:3

F. Motherhood is often devalued by the __culture__.

1. A successful mom can be defined by the choices she makes.

2. The "supermom" myth is unrealistic.

> *Encourage the young women ... to be sensible ...*
>
> Titus 2:5

II. Mom is a home builder.

> *She looks well to the ways of her household, and does not eat the bread of idleness.*
>
> Proverbs 31:27

A. Building a home is God's primary __call__ for a mom.

> *A wise woman builds her house, but the foolish tears it down with her own hands.*
>
> Proverbs 14:1

1. A mother's home is her __primary__ sphere of influence.

Handwritten margin notes:

Parenting Raising Teens w/ love + Logic (Foster & Klein)

Cleaning a house is like stringing beans w/out a knot in the end of it.

a. Much of her children's security and identity are developed at home.

b. Much of her children's future is shaped by her influence.

2. A mother's home ___reflects___ her values.

3. A mother's home ought to be a place of ___spiritual___ growth and encouragement.

B. Building a home requires that a couple depends upon the wisdom of God.

By wisdom a house is built, and by understanding it is established; and by knowledge the rooms are filled with all precious and pleasant riches.

Proverbs 24:3-4

1. A couple should prayerfully consider, then agree upon their motives and priorities before Mom becomes involved in too many activities outside the home.

a. Will additional activities outside the home compete with the child's need for nurturing and care?

b. Will her husband receive the love and attention he needs to succeed?

c. Is she emphasizing personal fulfillment through a career or outside activities instead of through her relationship with God and the dynamics of her family?

d. If the activity provides income, is the extra income essential to meet ___Needs___ or ___wants___?

2. There are "seasons" in a family when Mom's activities outside the home may be more ___appropriate___ than at other times.

a. Pre-children

b. Financial hardship due to circumstances beyond control

c. Empty nest

[handwritten margin notes: What's a mother's worth (13yrs ago) Sylvia Porter hourly wage for mom 23,000 - LA 24 K Chicago 28 K]

3. There are "seasons" when a family's needs could be

_____undermined_____ by Mom's distraction with too many outside activities.

    a. Young children

    b. Teenage years

    c. A husband will always need a supportive wife.

4. The _____attitude_____ a couple has about Mom's importance in the family will directly influence how the children value their mom and her role.

III. Mom is a lover of children.

... encourage the young women to love their husbands, to love their children ...

Titus 2:4

A. A mother's love is _____nurturing_____ .

But we proved to be gentle among you, as a nursing mother tenderly cares for her own children.

1 Thessalonians 2:7

Catch kids doing something right

B. A mother's love involves _____time_____ and attention.

pray for thsm + till thsm you do.

1. Children need to be a valued priority in a mother's heart.

2. Children need great amounts of time and attention to be healthy and well-adjusted.

C. A mother's love includes _____training_____ , instruction, correction, and discipline.

... a child who gets his own way brings shame to his mother ... correct your son, and he will give you comfort; he will also delight your soul.

Proverbs 29:15b, 17

D. God will honor a mother's love:

1. By blessing her

Her children rise up and bless her ...

Proverbs 31:28a

2. By blessing her children

The generation of the upright will be blessed.

Psalm 112:2b

IV. Mom is a teacher of children.

She opens her mouth in wisdom, and the teaching of kindness is on her tongue.

Proverbs 31:26

A. A mother teaches by communicating her values and priorities and by being a model that her children can pattern themselves after.

Train up a child in the way he should go, even when he is old he shall not depart from it.

Proverbs 22:6

B. A mother is the ___primary___ teacher of the next generation.

Hear ... your father's instruction, and do not forsake your mother's teaching.

Proverbs 1:8

1. She teaches her daughter about being a godly woman.

Charm is deceitful and beauty is vain, but a woman who fears the Lord, she shall be praised.

Proverbs 31:30

2. She models to her daughter the significant impact of her role as a wife and mother in God's design of the family.

3. She models to her son the kind of woman he should marry.

The sayings of King Lemuel, the oracle which his mother taught him.

Proverbs 31:1

4. She teaches her son how to honor and appreciate a woman's responsibilities of being a wife and mom.

5. She teaches and models to her children the importance of trusting in and living for Jesus Christ (1 Thessalonians 2:7-9).

Summary

A. A successful mom must be committed to God and His Word and not to the world.

1. She must spend time reading God's Word.

2. She must pray diligently for her husband and children.

3. This requires faith, courage, and perseverance.

B. Becoming a successful mom requires the power of God's Spirit to carry out the immense responsibilities of loving and nurturing children.

C. What kind of legacy will you, as a mother, leave?

The Wife's Responsibility for Oneness/Mom

Application Project

This application project has two sections: the individual section and the interaction section. Be sure to leave adequate time to interact as a couple on the interaction section.

Individual Section

35 Minutes

Setting: Find a place to be alone and complete this section.
Objective: Discover needs that you, your partner, and your children have.
Instructions: Complete both parts as instructed.

Part One:

1. Rate the statements on the chart below from 1 to 5.

STRONGLY DISAGREE					STRONGLY AGREE	Statement
1	2	3	④	5		The world's plan has distracted me from my responsibilities as a wife and mother.
1	②	3	4	5		My attitudes toward my husband reflect support and confidence in him.
1	②	3	4	5		My attitudes and actions toward my husband show him respect.
1	②	3	4	5		My attitudes and actions toward my husband show him love.
1	②	3	4	5		My attitude towards my husband reflects contentment and trust in God.
1	2	3	④	5		I am growing spiritually.
①	2	3	4	5		I support my husband's responsibility to initiate spiritually in our home.
①	2	3	4	5		I stay available to my husband with adequate time and energy.
1	②	3	4	5		My husband knows I admire him.
1	②	3	4	5		I am a positive encouragement to him.
1	②	3	4	5		I am a good friend of his.
①	2	3	4	5		I am willing to follow his direction for our home.
①	2	3	4	5		I accept him regardless of his performance.
1	2	③	4	5		I respect him.
1	②	3	4	5		I consider him my top priority.
1	2	③	4	5		I always back him up and verbally support him when we are in public.

STRONGLY DISAGREE						STRONGLY AGREE	
1	(2)	3	4	5			I express enjoyment in our sexual life.
(1)	2	3	4	5			I am spending consistent time in Bible study so I will be biblically accurate in my responsibilities as a wife and mother.
1	(2)	3	4	5			I communicate love and admiration for my husband in front of our children.
1	2	3	4	5			Biblical priorities are more important to me than status and lifestyle.
1	2	3	(4)	5			I save time and energy to nurture my children.
1	2	3	(4)	5			I model the character I want my children to emulate.
1	2	(3)	4	5			My home is a top priority.
(1)	2	3	4	5			I have regular communication with other mothers committed to biblical principles so I will be encouraged and accountable.

Part Two:

Answer the following questions.

1. What do you think your husband's five greatest needs are? How can you practically begin to meet them?

> sex
> companionship
> support
> commitment to our marriage
> someone to do fun things with
> be a good mom

2. What are your own five greatest needs as a wife and mother? How can your husband help provide leadership for you in these areas?

> be my best friend
> affection
> respect
> support
> understanding

3. What makes each of your children unique? List the two greatest needs of
    each child. How can you use these needs to draw your children closer to
    Christ?

Kassy

compassionate
caring
|

Travis

athletic
fun
active
loves to talk
lots of energy

Morgan

strong willed
eager to learn
social

Each wants time w/ mom in different ways
Morgan — needs to feel secure/safe

Travis — needs to have
appropr. outlets for energy
Kassy — needs support for
learning difficulties

Part Three:

Complete the following worksheet.

WIFE'S RESPONSIBILITY	List one action point that will help you improve in each area.
Love	sex
Support	be a good listener
Respect	provide words of praise — do in front of kids
MOM	
Home builder	Show more love, support, respect to George
Lover of children	provide more individual time less tati - more quality
Teacher of children	be better model Teach Travis value of mom & wife

Interaction Section

No Time Limit

Setting: Find a time to meet with your husband after you both have finished the individual section.

Objective: To raise your awareness of each other's needs.

Instructions:

1. Discuss your work on parts one and two of the individual sections.

2. Listen to him as he shares his part.

3. Write one point of action you will take individually, as a couple, or with others on the *Take It Home* page.

4. Then, record that Point of Action onto the *Take It Home Summary* flap on the back cover.

Take It Home

 I will do this! Check one or more of the following:

☐ Because the calling of motherhood is holy, I will find time each day to pray and to read God's Word.

☐ I will begin this week to renew my own thinking about the priority of motherhood. I will remind myself every day this month that:

☐ My children are a blessing, not a burden.

☐ Working to raise children who are spiritually strong and emotionally healthy is a vital vocation.

☐ My influence on the lives of my children will shape the future in a profound way.

☐ God will give me the wisdom and strength I need to do the job.

☐ I will reevaluate my other commitments and responsibilities outside my home to make sure my husband and my children are my priority.

☐ Because I have let my children become a higher priority than my husband, I will take steps this week to make sure my children know my relationship with my husband comes second only to my relationship with Christ.

☐ I will pray with my children each day and look for opportunities to teach them about God.

 Let's talk! We will discuss:

☐ Things I can do (from my husband's perspective) to be a better mom

☐ Specific character qualities we want to see cultivated in the life of each child

☐ How we can work together as a team in the spiritual training of our children

 Let's learn! I will read the following book:

☐ *A Mother's Legacy* compiled and written by Barbara Rainey and Ashley Rainey Escue

☐ *Different Children, Different Needs* by Charlie Boyd

☐ *Praying the Bible for Your Children* by David and Heather Kopp

☐ *So You're About to be a Teenager* by Dennis Rainey

10

The Husband's Responsibility for Oneness

The Husband's
Responsibility for Oneness

 Session 10 Overview

The fulfillment of a husband's role in marriage leads to oneness.

I. A husband is responsible to accept God's design for marriage.

A. God has designed a divine _____ of responsibility in marriage.

   1. God has designated the husband as the _____ of the relationship.

    For the husband is the head of the wife, as Christ is also the head of the church, He Himself being the Savior of the body.

   Ephesians 5:23

   2. God has given the wife to the husband to be his _____ in the relationship.

    Then the Lord God said, "It is not good for the man to be alone; I will make him a helper suitable for him."

   Genesis 2:18

B. God has designed the husband and the wife to be

_____ .

However in the Lord, neither is woman independent of man, nor is man independent of woman.

1 Corinthians 11:11

C. God has designed the husband and the wife with

_____ _____ .

There is neither Jew nor Greek, there is neither slave nor free man, there is neither male nor female, for you are all one in Christ Jesus.

Galatians 3:28

D. God has provided the husband and the wife the power to fulfill His design through dependence upon His Spirit.

"For apart from Me, you can do nothing."

John 15:5b

E. God has designed the husband-wife relationship to be a living picture of the relationship between Christ and the church.

CHRIST

CHERISHES
NOURISHES
SACRIFICES
WASHES
IN WORD
LOVES

CHURCH

II. Love like the Savior

Husbands, love your wives, just as Christ also loved the church and gave Himself up for her.

Ephesians 5:25

A. Love is seeking _____ best for our spouse.

1. Love is based on an act of the will, not passing feelings.

Husbands, love your wives, and do not be embittered against them.

Colossians 3:19

2. Love is sacrificial _____, not good intentions.

3. Love is given in obedience to Christ, not in response to our spouse's performance.

4. Love is expressed _____ and in actions.

5. Love involves self-denial.

   Note: When you love your wife sacrificially, you model the relationship between Christ and the church to your family and the world.

B. Love's goal is the building up and enrichment of a wife.

   So husbands ought also to love their own wives as their own bodies. He who loves his own wife loves himself; for no one ever hated his own flesh, but nourishes and cherishes it, just as Christ also does the church, because we are members of His body.

   Ephesians 5:28-30

1. A husband's love should _____ his wife by encouraging and enabling her to grow and develop her gifts and abilities.

2. A husband's love should cherish his wife by responding to her needs as a valued gift from God.

   a. A wife feels cherished when her husband

      _____ with her.

   b. A wife feels cherished when there is

      _____ in the relationship.

   c. A wife feels cherished when her husband

      is _____ .

   d. A wife feels cherished when her husband makes her load lighter, not heavier.

   "Come to Me, all who are weary and heavy-laden, and I will give you rest. Take My yoke upon you, and learn from Me, for I am gentle and humble in heart; and you shall find rest for your souls. For My yoke is easy, and My load is light."

   Matthew 11:28-30

e. A wife feels cherished when her husband prays with her and sets a godly example.

3. A husband's love should be expressed as he seeks to more fully _____ his wife.

You husbands likewise, live with your wives in an understanding way, as with a weaker vessel, since she is a woman; and grant her honor as a fellow heir of the grace of life, so that your prayers may not be hindered.

1 Peter 3:7

a. A wife feels understood when her husband

_____ with her in making key decisions.

b. A wife feels understood when her husband

_____ her needs, values, and preferences.

c. A wife feels understood when her husband

_____ without trying to fix her problems.

III. Lead like a servant

A. Leadership in marriage is based on_____ placement, not superior abilities.

But I want you to understand that Christ is the head of every man, and the man is the head of the woman, and God is the head of Christ.

1 Corinthians 11:3

B. Leadership in marriage is based on _____ example, not society.

"Rulers of the Gentiles lord it over them ... but it is not so among you, but whoever wishes to become great among you shall be your servant."

Mark 10:42-43

Have this attitude in yourselves which was also in Christ Jesus, who, although He existed in the form of God, did not regard equality with God a thing to be grasped, but emptied Himself, taking the form of a bond-servant, and being made in the likeness of men.

Philippians 2:5-7

C. Leadership includes providing for the material needs of your family.

But if anyone does not provide for his own, and especially for those of his household, he has denied the faith, and is worse than an unbeliever.

1 Timothy 5:8

1. A husband should sharpen his skills as a money manager (godly stewardship).

2. A husband should be aware of the material needs of his wife and his children.

D. Leadership involves taking the

_____ in meeting needs.

E. Leadership involves providing for

your wife's _____ needs.

1. A husband leads his wife spiritually through selfless service.

2. A husband leads his wife spiritually by modeling godly character.

3. A husband leads his wife spiritually by initiating time together in God's Word.

4. A husband leads his wife spiritually by regularly praying with her.

F. Caution: Abdicating or abusing your responsibilities as a husband to love, lead, and care for your wife is taken seriously by God.

" ... the Lord has been a witness between you and the wife of your youth, against whom you have dealt treacherously, though she is your companion and your wife by covenant. But not one has done so who has a remnant of the Spirit ... take heed then, to your spirit, and let no one deal treacherously against the wife of your youth."

Malachi 2:14-15

Note: A husband is never called to force his wife to follow his leadership. Rather, he is challenged to earn this response by being a man of integrity, compassion, and competence. Remember, a leader is a lover and a lover is a leader.

 **Summary**

A. Will you seek oneness with your wife:

   1. By accepting God's design for marriage?

   2. By loving your wife sacrificially?

   3. By accepting responsibility to lead in your marriage?

   4. By providing spiritual leadership in your marriage?

B. As you seek to understand your wife and attempt to meet her needs in loving ways, you will be able to lead with credibility and integrity and she will feel cared for and highly esteemed.

C. Remember, God has designed a husband and a wife to fulfill their roles and responsibilities through dependence on His Spirit and His Word.

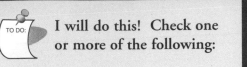

Take It Home

INDIVIDUAL APPLICATION   **COUPLE APPLICATION**

I will do this! Check one or more of the following:

☐ I will take the initiative to begin praying with my wife every day.

☐ I will find a resource that can help me with suggestions on ways I can affirm my wife (see the FamilyLife Resource Center for creative help in this area).

☐ I will memorize 1 Peter 3:7 by writing that verse on a 3 x 5 card and putting it on the dashboard of my car.

☐ Because I know that pornography dishonors my wife, I will take the following steps to be free from my struggle in this area:

   ☐ I will ask a mature Christian man to help hold me accountable in this area.

   ☐ I will tell my wife about my struggle with pornography and ask for her forgiveness and for accountability from her.

   ☐ I will get rid of any pornography in our home or on my computer's hard drive.

   ☐ I will read *Every Man's Battle* by Fred Stoeker.

☐ I will review the five ways a husband can cherish his wife on pages 148-149, and select one way I can show my wife this week that I cherish her.

Let's talk! We will discuss:

☐ Sometime in the next 30 days, I will ask my wife to answer the following five questions:

   ☐ What attribute would you like me to develop?

   ☐ What attribute would you like me to help you develop?

   ☐ What achievement in my life would bring you greatest joy?

   ☐ What would indicate to you that I really desire to be more Christ-like?

   ☐ What mutual goal would you like to see us accomplish?

☐ If my wife is working outside the home, should she continue? If not, how can we begin making plans so she can stay at home?

Let's learn! I will read the following book:

☐ *The Christian Husband* by Bob Lepine

☐ *Rocking The Roles* by Robert Lewis and William Hendricks

☐ *Four Pillars of a Man's Heart* by Stu Weber

10

Session Eleven

Dad

Dad

Session 11 Overview

The character of a dad has lasting influence on his children.

I. Dad

A. Dad is the leader of his family. He is a _____ .

B. Dad's heart helps him shepherd his family.

He is a _____ .

And he will restore the hearts of the fathers to their children, and the hearts of the children to their fathers, lest I come and smite the land with a curse.

Malachi 4:6

C. Dad's character provides the basis of how he

leads. He is a _____ .

Furthermore, you shall select out of all the people able men who fear God, men of truth, those who hate dishonest gain; and you shall place these over them, as leaders of thousands, of hundreds, of fifties, and of tens.

Exodus 18:21

II. Dad is the family manager.

A. He must _____ his household and keep his children under control.

He must be one who manages his own household well, keeping his children under control with all dignity ...

1 Timothy 3:4

B. Dad manages by being _____ dependent on God.

By wisdom a house is built, and by understanding it is established; and by knowledge the rooms are filled with all precious and pleasant riches.

Proverbs 24:3,4

1. He manages with knowledge.

Know well the condition of your flocks, and pay attention to your herds ...

Proverbs 27:23

2. He manages with understanding.

And, fathers, do not provoke your children to anger; but bring them up in the discipline and instruction of the Lord.

Ephesians 6:4

3. He manages with wisdom.

And guided them with his skillful hands.

Psalm 78:72b

But if any of you lacks wisdom, let him ask of God, who gives to all men generously and without reproach, and it will be given to him.

James 1:5

III. Dad is the family minister.

A. He _____ his flock.

Shepherd the flock of God among you, exercising oversight not under compulsion, but voluntarily, according to the will of God; and not for sordid gain, but with eagerness; nor yet as lording it over those allotted to your charge, but proving to be examples to the flock.

1 Peter 5:2-3

B. He ministers to his flock by caring for their

_____ .

1. He considers them a privilege to care for. (Voluntarily)

2. He makes them a priority. (Eagerness)

3. He leads them by being a model. (Example)

4. He provides for their needs. (Shepherd)

The Lord is my shepherd, I shall not want. He makes me lie down in green pastures; He leads me beside quiet waters. He restores my soul; He guides me in the paths of righteousness for His name's sake. Even though I walk through the valley of the shadow of death, I fear no evil; for Thou art with me; Thy rod and Thy staff, they comfort me. Thou dost prepare a table before me in the presence of my enemies; Thou has anointed my head with oil; my cup overflows. Surely goodness and lovingkindness will follow me all the days of my life, and I will dwell in the house of the Lord forever.

Psalm 23

5. He tells them he loves them. (Expressiveness)

IV. Dad is the family model.

A. Dad must _____ God's truth in his own life.

So he shepherded them according to the integrity of his heart ...

Psalm 78:72a

1. What a man is determines what a man does.

2. A man's character is shaped by his relationship with God.

3. A man's priorities are reshaped by the Word of God.

And do not be conformed to this world, but be transformed by the renewing of your mind, that you may prove what the will of God is, that which is good and acceptable and perfect.

Romans 12:2

B. Dad must _____ God's truth down through the generations.

BIBLICAL TIMES   1700s   1800s   2000s

For He established a testimony in Jacob, and appointed a law in Israel, which He commanded our fathers, that they should teach them to their children, that the generation to come might know, even the children yet to be born, that they may arise and tell them to their children, that they should put their confidence in God, and not forget the works of God, but keep His commandments.

Psalm 78:5-7

1. Dad must have the Word of God in his own heart.

Let the word of Christ richly dwell within you.

Colossians 3:16a

2. Dad uses daily opportunities to equip his children. He is diligent.

And these words, which I am commanding you today, shall be on your heart; and you shall teach them diligently to your sons and shall talk of them when you sit in your house and when you walk by the way and when you lie down and when you rise up. And you shall bind them as a sign on your hand and they shall be as frontals on your forehead. And you shall write them on the doorposts of your house and on your gates.

Deuteronomy 6:6-9

3. Dad structures formal teaching times to instruct his children.

Hear, O sons, the instruction of a father, and give attention that you may gain understanding, for I give you sound teaching; do not abandon my instruction.

Proverbs 4:1-2

V. Summary: What is a successful dad?

A. A successful dad must be gripped with the importance of his responsibility to his family. He needs time with his children.

B. A successful dad must ask God to do a work in his own heart. He needs God's Word to guide his life.

C. A successful dad must persevere as a leader by conquering fear and failure. He needs toughness in his heart.

D. What kind of legacy will you leave?

TEN TIPS FOR BEING AN EFFECTIVE DAD

1. When you get home, give your child a hug, a kiss, and the nodding approval that you believe in him and love him for who he is, not just for what he does.

2. Pray with your children. Don't be afraid to express your needs to God in prayer. Ask your children to pray for you.

3. On business trips, drop them a post card or note. Call them on extended trips.

4. Make up a story; read a story; tell them about your childhood.

5. Wrestle on the floor with them.

6. Set an evening aside in advance for a real, bona fide date with each child.

7. Write your grown children a letter to express your love. Maybe even a confession or two of how you wished you'd done more with them might be appropriate.

8. Touch them. Hold their hand. Run your fingers through their hair and express your appreciation to them.

9. Read the *Chronicles of Narnia* by C.S. Lewis to them.

10. Take a walk together. Just talk about the "stuff" of their lives.

II

The Husband's Responsibility for Oneness/Dad

Application Project

This application project has two sections: the individual section and the interaction section. Be sure to leave adequate time to interact as a couple on the interaction section.

Individual Section

35 Minutes

Setting: Find a place to be alone and complete this section.
Objective: Discover needs that you and your spouse have.
Instructions: Complete both parts as instructed.

Part One

STRONGLY DISAGREE					STRONGLY AGREE	
1 2 3 4 5						The world's plan has distracted me from my responsibilities as a husband and father.
1 2 3 4 5						My leadership style makes biblical submission easy and reasonable for my wife.
1 2 3 4 5						My leadership style makes my wife feel cherished and understood.
1 2 3 4 5						My leadership is characterized by taking the initiative.
1 2 3 4 5						My leadership style allows our home to be well-managed.
1 2 3 4 5						I verbalize acceptance and honor to my wife.
1 2 3 4 5						I show love for my wife with sacrificial action.
1 2 3 4 5						I demonstrate love even when I don't feel it.
1 2 3 4 5						I know my wife's needs.
1 2 3 4 5						I esteem my wife in her role as a wife (and mother).
1 2 3 4 5						I live with my wife in an understanding way.
1 2 3 4 5						I am growing spiritually.
1 2 3 4 5						My wife knows she is my top priority.
1 2 3 4 5						My wife knows that I need her.
1 2 3 4 5						My love for my wife models Christ's sacrificial love to my children.

STRONGLY DISAGREE					STRONGLY AGREE	
1	2	3	4	5		I initiate spiritual guidance to my children.
1	2	3	4	5		I model the character I want my children to emulate.
1	2	3	4	5		I use daily opportunities to equip and train my children.
1	2	3	4	5		I am aware of each of my children's unique needs.
1	2	3	4	5		I am spending consistent time studying the Bible so our family remains biblically accurate.
1	2	3	4	5		I make it a point to transfer the truth of God's Word to my children.
1	2	3	4	5		My children see me demonstrating sacrificial love for their mother.

2. Underline any of the statements from the previous chart that you feel need urgent change.

Part Two

Answer the following questions.

1. What do you think are your wife's five greatest needs? How can you practically begin to meet them?

2. What are your own five greatest needs as a husband and father? How can your wife be a helper to you?

3. What makes each of your children unique? List the two greatest needs of each child. In what way can you use these needs to point your children to a relationship with Christ?

Part Three

Complete the following worksheet.

HUSBAND'S RESPONSIBILITY	List one action point that will help you improve in each area.
Love	
Lead	

DAD	List one action point that will help you improve in each area.
Manager	
Minister	
Model	

Interaction Section
No Time Limit

Setting: Find a time to meet with your wife after you both have finished the individual sections.

Objective: To raise your awareness of each other's needs.

Instructions:

1. Discuss your work on parts one and two of the individual sections.

2. Listen to her as she shares her part.

3. Write one point of action you will take individually, as a couple, or with others on the *Take It Home* page.

4. Then, record that point of action onto the *Take It Home Summary* flap attached to the back cover.

Take It Home

INDIVIDUAL APPLICATION	COUPLE APPLICATION

I will do this! Check one or more of the following:

- [ ] I will take the initiative to begin leading our family in devotions.
- [ ] I will schedule at least one special event with each of my children, one on one, for each month.
- [ ] There is an area where I need to ask one of my children for his forgiveness. I will do that this week.
- [ ] Sometime over the next month, I will complete at least four of the following seven ideas for being a more effective dad:
  - [ ] Hug each of my children at least once a week and tell them I love them.
  - [ ] Pray with my children and ask them to pray for me about specific things.
  - [ ] Send them a card in the mail.
  - [ ] Read to them (*The Chronicles of Narnia* is a good choice!).
  - [ ] Wrestle on the floor with them.
  - [ ] Write a letter to an older child to express my belief in him.
  - [ ] Go for a walk together or go out for ice cream.

Let's talk! We will discuss:

- [ ] Things I can do (from my wife's perspective) to be a better dad
- [ ] Specific character qualities we would like to see developed in each child
- [ ] How and when we can have more regular times for family devotions

Let's learn! I will read the following book:

- [ ] *How To Be Your Daughter's Daddy/How To Be Your Little Man's Dad* by Dan Bolin and Ken Sutterfield
- [ ] *Four Pillars of a Man's Heart* by Stu Weber
- [ ] *Different Children, Different Needs* by Charlie Boyd
- [ ] *Raising A Modern Day Knight* by Robert Lewis
- [ ] *So You're About to be a Teenager* by Dennis Rainey

12

Resolving Conflict: Communication III

Resolving Conflict: Communication III

Session 12 Overview

*Resolution of conflict requires that a couple
lovingly confronts one another and is willing to seek and grant forgiveness.*

marriage made in heaven, so is thunder & lightening

I. Resolving conflict

Follow the rules
Females always make rules
can △
males can't remember all rules
if misunderstanding due to male
female can △ mind
Male can't unless ask

A. Conflict is common to all marriages. Therefore, the goal of marriage is not to be conflict-free, but to handle conflict correctly when it occurs.

uncontrolled anger

RT O
F H
LC A

O offend each other (intentional or not) little things bother us.
H hurt (natural tendency)
A anger

B. All marriages suffer from various degrees of pain and anger brought
on by a spouse's offense. Therefore, the first key to resolving

conflict is understanding the _____anatomy_____ of anger.

LC - Loving confrontation speak truth in love
F forgiveness - I'm sorry

C. The choices you make during a conflict will either drive you apart or
bind you together. Therefore, the second key to resolving conflict

RT ~ rebuild trust
is learning how to lovingly _____confront_____ your spouse.

D. When we fail to deal properly with conflict in our marriage, we move toward isolation. Therefore, the third key to resolving conflict requires that we learn how to seek and how to grant

_____forgiveness_____.

II. Resolving conflict requires understanding the anatomy of anger.

A. When we are hurt by our spouse, our natural tendency is to respond in one of two ways:

peace KEEPER at my expense
peace at any cost lose I

1. _____~~clam~~ sta//~~ff~~_____ it (rejection, withdrawal)

2. _____blow_____ it (anger, aggression, hostility) *tellers*
win the arguement—they think they are right
$1 worth of rage for 5¢ problem

B. For many people, anger is the most common response when conflict occurs.

Let everyone be quick to hear, slow to speak, and slow to anger.

James 1:19b

1. Why do we show anger?

a nation of finger pointers (she/them)

a. Our "rights" have been violated. *what rights do we really have. (Have right to be respected....)*

b. Our _____expectations_____ have not been met.

c. We have been _____hurt_____.

2. For some people, it's safer to show anger than to acknowledge hurt. *leaves you in control of conflict—don't have to figure out why you are hurt*

C. Anger is a God-given emotion. It can be a motivation to resolve conflict. *nerve endings on your soul*
invalid anger— when dignity of gods creation diminished, you have rt to to be angry

Be angry, and yet do not sin; do not let the sun go down on your anger. *↑ not literal acknowledge it*

Ephesians 4:26

12

D. Anger can be a very dangerous ___WEapoN___.

 Then the Lord said to Cain, "Why are you angry? And why has your countenance fallen? If you do well, will not your countenance be lifted up? And if you do not do well, sin is crouching at the door; and its desire is for you, but you must master it."

Genesis 4:6-7

E. Anger must be ___Controlled___. Uncontrolled anger can result in:

1. Bitterness that leads to resentment

2. Depression   *turn anger inward*

3. Conflict with God

4. Violence and even murder (Matthew 5:21-22)

F. Unresolved conflict can multiply the ___intensity___ of future conflicts.

UNRESOLVED CONFLICT LEADS TO ISOLATION

every brick an open loop

One Brick = One Choice

III. Resolving conflict requires loving confrontation.

> . . . but speaking the truth in love, we are to grow up in all aspects into Him, who is the head, even Christ . . .
>
> Ephesians 4:15

A. Speak the truth in ___love___ .

> Let no unwholesome word proceed from your mouth, but only such a word as is good for edification according to the need of the moment, that it may give grace to those who hear.
>
> Ephesians 4:29

B. Approach confrontation ___carefully___ .

> Brethren, even if a man is caught in any trespass, you who are spiritual *(mature)*, restore such a one in a spirit of gentleness; each one looking to yourself, lest you too be tempted.
>
> Galatians 6:1

12

FOCUS ON:	RATHER THAN:
One issue	Many issues
The problem	The person
Behavior	Character
Specifics	Generalizations
Expression of feelings	Judgment of character
"I" statements	"You" statements
Observation of facts	Judgment of motive
Mutual understanding	Who's winning or losing

1. Check your motivation.
   do you need to let it go
2. Check your attitude. *does it have to be correct*

3. Check the circumstances: timing, setting, other pressures.
   HALT - hungry, , lonely, tired don't talk to me then
4. Check to see if you're willing to accept confrontation as well as give it.

not blaming statements

C. Approach confrontation with ___prayer___ .

D. Agree on the way you will discuss resolving conflicts.

IV. Resolving conflict requires forgiveness.

And be kind to one another, tender-hearted, forgiving each other, just as God in Christ also has forgiven you.

Ephesians 4:32

A. The Bible teaches that all Christians are responsible to God to seek and grant forgiveness. → *takes change* *(38 yrs crippled - do you want healed - now have to go to work...)*

B. The offender needs to ___seek___ forgiveness. *No sorry in sorry unless admit wrong.*

SEEKING FORGIVENESS

1. Be willing to admit, "I am wrong."   "I was wrong. I shouldn't have _____."

2. Be willing to say, "I am sorry."   "I am sorry I did _____ and that I caused you to feel _____."

3. Be willing to repent.   "I know that I have hurt you deeply, and I do not wish to hurt you this way again."

4. Be willing to ask for forgiveness.   "Will you forgive me for doing _____?"

Not if I offended you, I'm sorry
I'm sorry but if ......

If therefore you are presenting your offering at the altar, and there remember that your brother has something against you, leave your offering there before the altar, and go your way; first be reconciled to your brother and then come and present your offering.

Matthew 5:23-24

C. The offended needs to ___grant___ *(give)* forgiveness.

1. Granting forgiveness is (not:)

   a. Repression or pretending that something did not happen or that it did not hurt   *Elephant in the living room.*

12

b. Conditional

Then Peter came and said to Him, "Lord, how often shall my brother sin against me and I forgive him? Up to seven times?" Jesus said to him, "I do not say to you, up to seven times, but up to seventy times seven."

Matthew 18:21-22

c. Forgetting

d. _____ . "I can't forgive you" really means, "I'm not ready to forgive you," or "I won't forgive you."

e. An automatic cure for the hurt

2. Granting forgiveness is:

a. Obedience to a command

... bearing with one another, and forgiving each other, whoever has a complaint against anyone; just as the Lord forgave you, so also should you.

Colossians 3:13

[handwritten: set you free when you forgive you set the prisoner free only to recognize you were the prisoner]

b. An _____ of letting go of resentment and my right to get even

c. An _____ that must be expressed by word and deed

d. A _____ to set your spouse free from a debt or an offense that has occurred against you

e. The beginning of the healing process that leads to oneness

12

GRANTING FORGIVENESS

1. Do it privately first: "God, I forgive _____ for hurting me."

2. Do it specifically: "I forgive you for _____."

3. Do it generously: "Let's settle this issue and get on with building our relationship."

4. Do it graciously: "I know I've done things like that myself."

V. The Process of Reconciliation

A. Forgiveness begins the process by which _____ can be rebuilt.

   1. The offending partner must take the _____ in rebuilding trust.

   2. The offended partner must _____ the natural tendency to rehearse the hurt.

B. Discuss specific solutions to the problem.

   1. What do we do about the hurt we still feel?

   2. What do we change so that this situation does not occur again?

   3. What do we do if we still disagree?

C. Seeking and granting forgiveness in this way restores oneness.

THE SEVEN As OF FORGIVENESS

Address everyone involved (Proverbs 28:13; 1 John 1:8-9)

Avoid if, but, and maybe (don't make excuses; Luke 15:11-24)

Admit specifically (both attitudes and actions)

Apologize (express sorrow for the way you affected someone)

Accept the consequences (Luke 19:1-9)

Alter your behavior (commit to changing harmful habits; Ephesians 4:22-32)

Ask for forgiveness

Taken from *The Peacemaker* by Ken Sande. Used by permission.

12

 **VI.** **Summary**

A. Unresolved conflict leads to isolation.

B. Will you choose to handle conflict constructively?

C. Remember: God's power is available to you when you are willing to seek or grant forgiveness.

RESOLVED CONFLICT RESULTS IN ONENESS

One Brick = One Choice

Resolving Conflict
Application Project

This application project has two sections: the individual section and the interaction section. Be sure to leave adequate time to interact as a couple on the interaction section.

Individual Section

25 Minutes

Setting: Stay together as a couple, but complete this section quickly without any interaction.

Objective: To begin the process of practicing forgiveness.

Instructions: Complete both parts of this section.

Part One

1. Select one unresolved or recurring conflict where you have hurt your spouse, and write it down on a separate piece of paper.

2. How does your spouse respond when you have hurt or offended him?

3. How do you respond when you have offended him?

4. Are you willing to ask your spouse to forgive you?

Part Two

Prepare your heart by humbling yourself before God. Confess any anger that may keep "the wall" up and your spouse at a distance. Thank God that He has forgiven you (read 1 John 1:8-9). Then, acknowledge your willingness before God to seek forgiveness from your spouse. Likewise, prepare your heart to grant forgiveness to your spouse by thanking God for him.

Therefore, confess your sins to one another, and pray for one another, so that you may be healed. The effective prayer of a righteous man can accomplish much.

James 5:16

Interaction Section

20-30 Minutes

Setting: Stay together for interaction.

1. Make sure you are able to talk freely.

2. Don't be defensive. Acknowledge your contribution to problems.

3. Concentrate on using "I" statements only. Avoid words like "if," "but," "maybe," "you never," or "you always."

4. Seek to listen.

5. Express the truth in love.

Objective: To verbally seek or grant forgiveness with your spouse.

Instructions:

Step 1

1. Husband:

   a. Share with your wife the answers listed in Part One of the individual section.

   b. While looking at your wife, restate the offense you would like to seek forgiveness for and ask her forgiveness.

2. Wife:

    a. Grant forgiveness to your husband with your words. Be honest.

    b. Then, by deed, take the offense written down on the piece of paper and throw it away or burn it as a symbolic gesture of the freedom forgiveness grants.

Step 2

1. Wife:

    a. Share with your husband the answers listed in Part One of the individual section.

    b. While looking at your husband, restate the offense you would like to seek forgiveness for and ask his forgiveness.

2. Husband:

    a. Grant forgiveness to your wife with your words. Be honest.

    b. Then, by deed, take the offense written down on the piece of paper and throw it away or burn it as a symbolic gesture of the freedom forgiveness grants.

Step 3

Write one point of action you will take individually, as a couple, or with others on the *Take It Home* page.

Step 4

Then, record that point of action onto the *Take It Home Summary* flap attached to the back cover.

Take It Home

I will do this! Check one or more of the following:

☐ Because my anger fuels much of the conflict in our marriage, I will:

☐ Talk with someone to help uncover the "hidden hurt" behind my anger.

☐ I will memorize the following verses from the Bible about anger: Proverbs 14:29, Proverbs 15:1, Proverbs 16:32, Proverbs 19:11, Ephesians 4:26, Ephesians 4:31, Colossians 3:8, James 1:19-20.

☐ During our next conflict, I will work hard to follow the suggestions for how to resolve conflict found on page 169.

☐ There is something I need to ask my spouse to forgive me for. I will review and practice the pattern outlined on page 170 so I can seek my spouse's forgiveness the right way.

☐ I need to forgive my spouse for something he or she has done in the past. I will review the information found on page 171, and will start moving toward granting forgiveness.

Let's talk! We will discuss:

☐ A specific area of regular conflict. We will agree to work through the project that begins on page 174 to practice how to resolve this conflict in a healthy, biblical manner.

☐ Controlling our conflict. When our emotions become intense in conflict, we should agree to at least a 10-minute "cooling off" period.

☐ How we can do a better job of focusing on a single issue in the midst of conflict?

☐ Helping one another remember that "my spouse is not my enemy," even when we're in conflict!

Let's learn! We will read the following book together:

☐ *Dr. Rosberg's Do It Yourself Relationship Mender* by Gary Rosberg

☐ *The Peacemaker* by Ken Sande

☐ *Resolving Conflict in Your Marriage* (HomeBuilders Couples Series® study guide) by Bob and Jan Horner

12

13

Resolving Conflict Through the Power of Blessing: Communication IV

Resolving Conflict II: The Power of Blessing

Session 13 Overview

Learn how to become a better lover instead of a bitter fighter.

I. The power of blessing

A. Understanding comes as we are quick to listen and careful in how we express ourselves as God's Word instructs us.

B. Real intimacy comes as we balance commitment, companionship, passion, and spiritual oneness as God has designed us.

C. Conflicts are resolved as we learn to control our anger, to lovingly confront each other, and to willingly seek and grant forgiveness as God has empowered us.

D. God Himself will care for us when we choose to respond to an insult by blessing another person as Jesus has modeled for us.

II. Giving a blessing

A. Giving a blessing begins with cultivating a new attitude toward your spouse.

13

To sum up, let all be harmonious, sympathetic, brotherly, kindhearted, and humble in spirit.

1 Peter 3:8

1. Harmony – *like minded, but different*

2. Sympathy – *feeling the same feeling listen to feelings, don't fix 'em*

3. Brotherliness – *close companionship – you like me – I like you*

4. Kindheartedness – *being kind*

I care & I'm listening don't blab keep private

5. Humility – *gear myself as God sees it (not more or less)*

"Discovering God's purpose for your life" Dick Purnell

B. The result of this attitude in a marriage relationship

is ___ONENESS___ .

III. The Scripture contrasts two kinds of marriage relationships.

Sarcasism – little bit of truth with a dig at the end.

Not returning evil for evil, or insult for insult, but giving a blessing instead.

1 Peter 3:9

A. The ___insult___ – ___for___ – ___insult___ relationship.

1. This is defined as: ___meaning to hurt by action or word___ .

2. This relationship is rooted in an ___unforgiving___ and hardened ___heart___ (attitude).

3. The insult-for-insult relationship has its focus on

"my ___rights___" and

"my ___feelings___."

humor – laugh with each other and not at each other

4. It is illustrated by the behavior of hiding and hurling. *(like snow ball!)*

13

5. One of the problems associated with the insult-for-insult relationship is reacting to your spouse's insult out of habit. (What situation do you tend to find yourself in when you're in an insult-for-insult relationship?)

B. The blessing-for-insult relationship → concrets or usrbal action that benefits the other

1. It is defined as: responding kindly when offended.

2. It is illustrated by the behavior of responding with pass on grace kindness, not reacting in anger.

3. This relationship is based on an attitude of forgiveness.

It takes more faith to forgive than to raise the dead

4. The blessing-for-insult relationship has its focus on God and the promises of His Word.

5. All of God's power is available to me when I entrust myself to the Father.

And while being reviled, He (Jesus) did not revile in return; while suffering, He uttered no threats, but kept entrusting Himself to Him who judges righteously.

1 Peter 2:23

IV. Three benefits of the blessing relationship

For you were called for the very purpose that you might inherit a blessing. For, "Let him who means to love life and see good days refrain his tongue from evil and his lips from speaking guile. And let him turn away from evil and do good; let him seek peace and pursue it. For the eyes of the Lord are upon the righteous, and His ears attend to their prayer, but the face of the Lord is against those who do evil."

1 Peter 3:9b-12

A. You will inherit a _blessing_ .   *what you sew, you reap*

B. You will have a full _life_ .

C. You will learn what it means to _walk_ with God.

For you have been called for this purpose, since Christ also suffered for you, leaving an example for you to follow in His steps, who committed no sin, nor was any deceit found in His mouth ...

1 Peter 2:21-22

be ths kind of person that you would like to marry

V. The Scriptures explain how to give a blessing (1 Peter 3:9b-12).

A. Refrain your tongue from speaking evil.   *touch- match that lights the forest fire*

B. Turn away from evil.   *watch your ~~words~~ thoughts because it becomes your ...*
words / actions / character   *actions / character / destiny*

C. Do good.

D. Seek to be a peacemaker, not a troublemaker.

13

VI. Summary

A. The blessing relationship is more an attitude of your heart than simply words from your lips. YOUR ATTITUDE IS CRUCIAL.

B. Remember, God's power is available to you when you must choose between responding to an insult with an insult or with a blessing.

C. What kind of relationship will you seek to maintain with your spouse?

Dick Purnell.com

Take It Home

INDIVIDUAL APPLICATION

I will do this! Check one or more of the following:

- ☐ I will review the five attitudes listed on page 181, and determine which of the five I need to cultivate.

- ☐ By faith, I will choose to respond with kindness and with a blessing the next time my spouse hurts me with his attitude or words.

- ☐ I will memorize 1 Peter 3:10-11 and follow that pattern the next time there is conflict with my spouse.

- ☐ I will examine my own heart to see if there are actions from the past where I have not completely forgiven my spouse (remember: forgiveness means giving up the right to punish someone who has wronged you).

- ☐ Because I tend to the be person in our marriage who most often gets angry or insults my spouse, I will ask my spouse to help me realize when I am angry or insulting.

- ☐ I will remind myself every day this week that "My spouse is not my enemy."

COUPLE APPLICATION

Let's talk! We will discuss:

- ☐ The time of day, location and/or situation where we tend to fall into the habit or pattern of "insult for insult"

- ☐ How we can help each other recognize and break the pattern

- ☐ Any words we may have spoken to each other over the years that have deeply wounded the other

- ☐ Never using the "D" word (divorce) with each other as a threat

Let's learn! We will read the following book together:

- ☐ *The Five Love Needs of Men and Women* by Gary and Barb Rosberg

13

14

Leaving a Legacy of Destiny

Leaving a Legacy of Destiny

Session 14 Overview

Leaving a godly legacy
requires character, commitment, and vision.

---

inspiration   In Flander's Field
                    John mc Crady

I. Leaving a legacy of destiny

David williams
off. lineman
Houston oiler—
gave up 1/16 of pay
to be there for
son's birth

A. Building a legacy brings many benefits.

Indeed, my heritage is beautiful for me!

Psalm 16:6b

Teddy Stalard

B. Leaving a legacy requires increasing levels of commitment.

1. Commit to growing in personal spiritual maturity.

"Abide in Me, and I in you. As the branch cannot bear fruit
of itself, unless it abides in the vine, so neither can you, unless
you abide in Me."

John 15:4

2. Commit to growing in love for one another.

"This is My commandment, that you love one another, just as I
have loved you."

John 15:12

3. Commit to helping reach the world with God's plan.

"When the Helper comes, whom I will send to you from the Father, that is the Spirit of truth, who proceeds from the Father, He will bear witness of Me."

John 15:26

C. Leaving a legacy requires finding our greatest joy in fulfilling God's will for our lives, marriages, and families.

II. Leaving a legacy of destiny requires pursuing personal growth in Christ.

A. Press on to growth in your relationship with Jesus Christ.

I urge you therefore, brethren, by the mercies of God, to present your bodies a living and holy sacrifice, acceptable to God, which is your spiritual service of worship. And do not be conformed to this world, but be transformed by the renewing of your mind, that you may prove what the will of God is, that which is good and acceptable and perfect.

Romans 12:1-2

Don't be squeezed into the world's mold –

B. As you go home, reality will challenge your commitment to Christ.

For our struggle is not against flesh and blood, but against the rulers, against the powers, against the world forces of this darkness, against the spiritual forces of wickedness in heavenly places.

Ephesians 6:12

1. Persist through the attacks from Satan, the flesh, and the world.

2. Persist through the discouragement caused by a lack of immediate results due to unrealistic expectations.

3. Don't wait for your spouse to act. Do what God expects of you.

take small steps

C. God will honor your faithfulness.

His master said to him, "Well done, good and faithful slave; you were faithful with a few things, I will put you in charge of many things; enter into the joy of your master."

Matthew 25:23

14

III. Leaving a legacy of destiny requires developing a godly family.

A. The family is God's smallest battle formation.

B. God's plan is in opposition to the world's plan.

	WORLD'S PATTERN	GOD'S PLAN
Perspectives on Marriage		
Orientation	Self	God
Motivation	Gratify self	Glorify God
Method	Promote self	Promote oneness

Purposes for Marriage	Have own needs met
	Achieve romantic dream
	   (live happily ever after)
	Sex
	Escape
		Mirror God's image
		Mutually complete
		   one another
		Multiply godly legacy

Plan	50/50 performance
	relationship
	"It'll never happen to me"
	   syndrome
	Based on feelings
	Conditional commitment
	   and acceptance
	Conflicting roles
		Responsibility before God to:
		   Accept completely
		   Establish interdependence
		   Establish commitment
		   Establish intimacy
		   Establish roles

Power	Flesh	God's Spirit
Results	Tribute to self Turmoil and division	Tribute to God Peace and harmony
	ISOLATION	**ONENESS**

C. God has equipped us with spiritual armor as we face our battle (Ephesians 6:10-18).

1. Identify and apply God's principles that are most strategic to your family.

2. Will you reaffirm your commitment to each other and dedicate your marriage to God by signing the marriage covenant?

D. Your family affects future generations.

IV. Leaving a legacy of destiny requires reaching out to the world and results in changing the world.

A. God wants to work through your family to help fulfill the Great Commission.

> *"Go therefore and make disciples of all the nations, baptizing them in the name of the Father and the Son and the Holy Spirit, teaching them to observe all that I commanded you; and lo, I am with you always, even to the end of the age."*
>
> Matthew 28:19-20

> *"But you shall receive power when the Holy Spirit has come upon you; and you shall be My witnesses both in Jerusalem, and in Judea and Samaria, and even to the remotest part of the earth."*
>
> Acts 1:8

Don't stop Don't quite Don't quite keep going

B. The reality of Jesus Christ in your marriage is attractive to others. You can reach others for Christ by sharing the principles you've learned this weekend.

C. You will find your greatest joy in life as you commit yourself to God's purposes for your life.

V. Summary

A. What kind of legacy will you leave?

B. Come help change the world by building a legacy of destiny.

14

Take It Home

 I will do this! Check one or more of the following:

☐ I will plan a time or event in the next 30 days when my spouse and I can share with our children how we became Christians.

☐ I will begin this week to cultivate new habits that will help me grow spiritually. This will include some or all of the following:

  ☐ Reading my Bible each day

  ☐ Praying each day

  ☐ Joining a local church, and actively participating in worship and service

  ☐ Sharing my faith in Christ with others

☐ In the next month, we will find a special time to sign our "Oneness Covenant." We will frame it and hang it in our home as a reminder of our commitment to each other.

☐ We will invite four other couples we know to come to our house to talk about starting a HomeBuilders group.

☐ We will make plans now to attend the FamilyLife "Weekend To Remember" again next year, and to bring other couples with us.

 Let's talk! We will discuss:

☐ How our family can be more involved together in sharing Christ with others

☐ How we can best hold each other accountable for growing in our relationship with Christ

☐ How we might join with FamilyLife in effectively developing godly families, as volunteers, donors, or full-time staff members

 Let's learn! We will read the following book together:

☐ *One Home At A Time* by Dennis Rainey

14

Appendices

Appendix A

Appendix B

Appendix C

Appendix D

Appendix E

Appendix A

Male/Female Differences

Men and women are physically different.

1. Men and women differ in every cell of their bodies. This difference in the chromosome combination is the basic cause of development into maleness or femaleness.

2. Women have greater constitutional vitality, perhaps because of this chromosome difference. In the United States women normally outlive men by three or four years.

3. The sexes differ in their basal metabolism—that of a woman being normally lower than that of a man.

4. They differ in skeletal structure, women having a shorter head, broader face, less protruding chin, shorter legs, and longer trunk. The first finger of a woman's hand is usually longer than the third; with men the reverse is true. Boys' teeth last longer than do those of girls.

5. A woman has a larger stomach, kidneys, liver, and appendix, and a woman has smaller lungs.

6. Women have several very important functions that are totally lacking in men: menstruation, pregnancy, and lactation, for example. All of these influence behavior and feelings. Women have different hormones from men. The same gland behaves differently in the two sexes—thus a woman's thyroid is larger and more active; it enlarges during pregnancy but also during menstruation; it makes her more prone to goiter, provides resistance to cold, and is associated with a smooth skin, a relatively hairless body, and a thin layer of subcutaneous fat, which are important elements in the concept of personal beauty. It also contributes to emotional instability—she laughs and cries more easily.

7. Women's blood contains more water, but 20 percent fewer red cells. Since red cells supply oxygen to the other body cells, she tires more easily and is more prone to faint. Her constitutional viability is therefore strictly a long-range matter. When the working day in British factories was increased from 10 to 12 hours under wartime conditions, accidents of women increased 150 percent, but of men not at all.

8. In brute strength, men are 50 percent stronger than women.

9. A woman's heart beats more rapidly (80 beats vs. 72 beats for men); blood pressure (10 points lower than a man's); varies from minute to minute; but she has much less tendency to high blood pressure—at least until after menopause.

10. A woman's vital capacity, or breathing power, is lower in the 7:10 ratio.

11. A woman stands high temperature better than a man does; metabolism slows down less.

From the article: "Are Women Really Different?", Dr. Paul Popenoe, *Family Life,* February 1971.

1. The woman's immunization system is more complex. She produces more immunoglobulin M. Her estrogen protects her from heart disease.

2. Males have a greater infant mortality rate.

   ◆ More males are spontaneously aborted and are born dead.

   ◆ Thirty percent more males die within the first month.

   ◆ Thirty-three percent more males have birth defects.

   ◆ Five times as many males have language disability and stutter.

3. Females mature faster than males.

4. Females are chemically and biologically more adapted to child bearing and child rearing.

5. Males are more chemically and biologically adapted to hunting and providing.

From the article: "Is There A Superior Sex?", Jo Durden-Smith and Diane De Simone, *Reader's Digest*, November 1982.

Men and women are different mentally and psychologically.

1. Verbal and spatial abilities in boys tend to be 'packaged' into different hemispheres: The right hemisphere for non-verbal tasks, the left for verbal tasks. But in girls non-verbal and verbal skills are likely to be found on both sides of the brain. This affects their actions and reactions.

2. From shortly after birth, females are more sensitive to certain types of sounds, particularly to a mother's voice, but also to loud noises.

3. Girls have more skin sensitivity, particularly in the fingertips, and are more proficient at fine motor performance.

4. Girls are more attentive to social contexts—faces, speech patterns, and subtle vocal cues.

5. Girls speak sooner, have larger vocabularies, rarely demonstrate speech defects, exceed boys in language abilities, and learn foreign languages more easily.

6. Boys show early visual superiority.

7. Boys have better total body coordination but are poorer at detailed hand activity, such as stringing beads.

8. Boys have different "attentional mechanisms" and react as quickly to inanimate objects as to a person.

9. Boys are more curious about exploring their environment.

10. Boys are better at manipulating three-dimensional space. They can mentally rotate or fold an object better.

11. Of 11 subtests for psychological measurements in "...the most widely used general intelligence test, only two (digit span and picture arrangement) reveal similar mean scans for males and females. There are six differences so consistent that the standard battery of this intelligence test now contains a masculinity-femininity index to offset sex-related proficiencies and deficiencies."

12. Girls who are "assertive and active" and can control events have greater intellectual development, while these factors are not as significant in male intellectual development.

13. More boys are hyperactive ("...more than 90 percent of hyperactives are male.")

14. Because the male brain is "primarily visual" and learns by manipulating its environment, listening instruction for boys in early elementary grades is more stressful for them. Girls therefore tend to exceed them.

15. Girls do less well on scholarship tests that are more geared for male performance at higher grades.

Data gathered by Dr. Richard Restak, Neurologist at Georgetown University School of Medicine.

1. Women have greater individual mood fluctuation. One in four women is seriously affected in pre-menstruation. Also at this time, women are inclined toward more illness, more tension, and show more inclination to crime.

2. There are more males at both ends of the intellectual spectrum—more retardates as well as more geniuses.

From the article: "Is There a Superior Sex?" Jo Durden-Smith and Diane De Simone, *Reader's Digest*, November 1982.

A Word From FamilyLife

Each year, millions of women are abused in the one place they thought they would be safe ... their homes. We have created this resource with two purposes:

- ◆ *To give abused women hope that their lives can change and*
- ◆ *To provide some concrete suggestions for how to move toward recovery.*

This is not a comprehensive study or a complete guide on domestic violence; nor does this provide all the necessary answers and help you will need. Our aim in writing this mini-book is to help you understand what is going on in your relationship, to give you some insight into what domestic violence is about, and to provide you with some guidance on how to change and rebuild your life and marriage.

This resource includes several large sections adapted with permission from resources developed by people who have experience and expertise in the area of domestic violence. However, quoting from these materials does not mean we endorse those materials in their entirety.

For the sake of simplicity, we have chosen to use the word "husband" when we refer to the abuser. We realize many victims of abuse are single, and that a growing number of men are abused by their wives. Please read through the material knowing that you may need to adapt it to your specific circumstances.

Some of you also may be reading this mini-book because you know someone in an abusive situation and you want to help. This material will give you important information that would help you be a supportive friend during this difficult time in her life. You will gain a better understanding about what is happening to your friend, what domestic violence and battering is all about, and how you can best help her. You may then want to pass this mini-book on to your friend, or walk through the material with her step by step.

It is our prayer that this mini-book excerpt will be a way of hope for you.

Appendix B

A Way of Hope

Seven Steps Toward Breaking the Cycle of Violence in Your Life

Step One: Recognize the Need for Change
Step Two: Understand That Healthy Relationships Have Boundaries
Step Three: Seek Outside Help and Guidance
Step Four: Determine the Level of Danger and Develop a Safety Plan
Step Five: Move Toward Personal Recovery by Establishing a Strong Relationship with God
Step Six: Encourage Your Husband to Get Help
Step Seven: Move Toward Reconciliation

STEP ONE: RECOGNIZE THE NEED FOR CHANGE

Sara's Story

The following is a true story, but details have been changed to protect the woman who tells it:

I was 17 years old, and about to enter my senior year of high school. I met Kurt, a terrific guy who thought I was "perfect," and we started dating. I thought I was in love.

Kurt lived a couple of hours away, so it was a long-distance relationship (I'm sure my parents were thankful). We talked on the phone every Wednesday for an hour or so. Some weekends, my parents would allow him to spend the weekend at our house with strict rules in force. I was always very obedient and knew not to step out of line.

My first indication that he had a temper was during a phone conversation one Wednesday. Kurt and his dad had just had a fight and he told me he had put his fist through his bedroom wall. When I told my mom about this, her comment was, "If he's hitting walls today, he might be hitting you tomorrow." I told her he would never do that because he loved me too much.

We were married three weeks after my high school graduation. My parents were devastated that I was not attending college; it had been their dream and mine for years. I had never had any real confidence in my abilities and practically no self-esteem. So I took the easy way out.

Soon, I noticed that my new husband was extremely jealous and protective. He accused me of sleeping with his friends. He would not allow me to visit my family; he seemed to feel threatened when anyone took attention away from him. When my parents would come into town to visit, he wouldn't allow me to go shopping with my mom or spend time with them. He didn't allow me to go anywhere without him and only he could drive our vehicle.

Even worse, I was becoming afraid of him. He had begun to fly into rages for no apparent reason. Up to this point, the worst that had happened were horrible arguments and lots of tears. Every outburst was followed by flowers and apologies that he wouldn't do it again.

Then I found out I was pregnant. Kurt seemed so happy and anxious. Then within a few months it seemed that all hell broke loose. It started one day as we were driving. He said this child couldn't be his, that he knew I had been with someone else, then he began screaming and calling me names. Then his fist seemed to come out of nowhere—hitting me in the stomach! I remember grabbing my stomach, doubling over, and moaning out loud. I was terrified that he had hurt the baby and I really couldn't believe what had just happened.

Kurt immediately pulled off the road and tried to hug me as his tears flowed. He kept asking me to forgive him, and he promised it would never happen again. I was hurting so bad I just wanted to die.

He kept his word for a few weeks. But then he flew into a rage one night and began throwing things and breaking anything in his path. This continued off and on until our son was born. Then life truly became a living hell.

The rages were even more frequent; now Kurt was convinced that I was sleeping with my coworkers. Nothing I said could convince him that I wasn't. The physical abuse really began at this point. I tried to cover the bruises with makeup or with long sleeves. I was so afraid my coworkers would find out and I couldn't bear the embarrassment.

Kurt began calling me at work to "check up on me." Then he started missing work and sitting in the adjoining parking lot so he could watch my office building. I felt alone and confused. I wanted to tell my parents, but I was afraid they wouldn't understand.

One night we went to the store and were bringing groceries in when something set him off. I was bringing our son in from the car when Kurt attacked me and shoved me down the stairs. I lost my balance and fell backward with Michael in my arms. I was trying to hold onto him with one arm and trying to stop us with the other. Finally, about halfway down, we landed and blood was everywhere. By the grace of God, our son's arm was only scratched, but my leg and knee were gashed.

I told Kurt that I would kill him if he ever laid another hand on me when our son was nearby. Kurt began crying, apologizing, and begging me to forgive him. I was repulsed by what I saw in him and what I saw in myself. I remember crying out to God and asking Him to protect my son and me.

You Are Not Alone

Your story may not sound exactly like the one you just read, but perhaps you can relate in some ways to her experience. When you are abused, you feel desperately alone. You may think, *Why me? Other women don't have this problem. Something must be wrong with me.* And you may feel so ashamed that this is happening to you that you don't want anyone to know about it. But the truth is that many wives suffer some form of domestic abuse regardless of racial, religious, educational, or economic backgrounds.

According to the American Medical Association, husbands and boyfriends severely assault as many as four million women every year. One in four women will experience some type of spousal abuse during their lifetime.[1] Many of these women feel trapped, anxious, afraid, and helpless. Some feel they are to blame—that if they could just do better at pleasing their husbands, they could change their situations. Others don't know what to do, or where to go to get help. Most suffer in silence, hiding their situations from family and friends because of the shame and embarrassment they feel. Or perhaps they fear others will not believe them.

No, you are not alone. But there is hope! Many women have taken bold and courageous steps to seek help, to find freedom from abuse, and to begin the journey toward a new life. Some have even seen their abusers find the help they desperately needed to stop their destructive behavior and to experience healing and recovery in their own lives. Some couples, through the help of intervention and a structured recovery process guided by pastors or qualified counselors, have been able to experience healing and reconciliation in their marriages.

Yes, it is true that change does take time, a lot of courage, and a great deal of support, but change *can* happen. And if you are in an abusive situation, change *must* happen.

What is Abuse?

A crucial first step in this process will be to acknowledge and understand the abuse occurring in your marriage. Abuse means to *mistreat* or *misuse* someone. People abuse others to dominate or control, or to prevent others from making free choices.

There are several different forms of abuse:

◆ *Emotional or psychological abuse*: Mistreating and controlling someone through fear, manipulation, and intimidation, and by attacking that person's sense of self-worth. The abuser seeks to make his wife feel afraid, helpless, confused, and worthless. This form of abuse includes: name-calling, mocking, belittling, accusing, blaming, yelling, swearing, harassing, isolating from family and friends, abusing authority, withholding emotional support and affection, and betraying trust.

◆ *Physical abuse*: Assaulting, threatening, or restraining a person through force. Men who batter use physical violence to control women—to scare them into doing whatever they want them to do. Physical abuse includes: hitting, slapping, punching, beating, grabbing, shoving, biting, kicking, pulling hair, burning, using or threatening the use of weapons, blocking you from leaving a room or the house during an argument, driving recklessly, or intimidating you with threatening gestures.

◆ *Sexual abuse*: Behavior that dominates or controls someone through sexual acts, demands or insults. Sexual abuse includes: making you do sexual things when it is against your will, when you are sick, or when it is painful; using force (including rape in or out of marriage), threats, or coercion to obtain sex or perform sexual acts; forcing you to have unprotected sex, or sex with others; treating you like a sex object, and calling you names like "frigid" or "whore."

Facing the Facts ... And Facing Your Fears

Denying the abuse or the impact of abuse may have helped you to cope with the problem until now. However, denial is also the very thing that will hinder you from breaking the cycle of violence in your life, and from experiencing peace and freedom from abuse. The fact that you are reading this mini-book is evidence that you are willing to acknowledge the abuse. You've already taken a courageous step.

Facing the fact that you are being abused or battered by your husband, and that his behavior is not normal, can stir up deep emotional feelings—especially fear. You must acknowledge these fears in order to face and deal with the problem. In her book, *Invisible Wounds—A Self-Help Guide for Women in Destructive Relationships*, Kay Douglas writes, "Unacknowledged fears play on our minds and sap our confidence until we have no energy left to deal with the problems at hand. The way out of fear is through it." She goes on to say, "As we face and feel our vulnerability, our fear may increase in intensity for a brief time. Then it begins to diminish. When we know what we are dealing with, much of the power of that feeling goes. We move through fear to a calmer, stronger place within. Having faced the worst, we are free to put our energy into coping creatively with our situation."[6]

It's Time to Make the Right Choices

You do not deserve to be abused, nor are you to blame for the abuse that you have suffered. Abuse of any type is wrong, and if you are in an abusive situation, the first step toward new life and freedom is to recognize that there is a need for a change in your life. Change can be difficult, and in some cases, change can be frightening. However, in any type of an abusive situation, change is absolutely necessary for your own well being.

Remember, abuse is about power and control. You may be experiencing verbal or emotional abuse now. But if changes are not made to resolve your current situation, then when your husband begins feeling as if he still does not have enough control, the abuse will escalate into more violent forms. According to the Metro Nashville Police Domestic Violence Division, "When abusers hit or break objects or make threats, almost 100 percent resort to physical battering."[7] What might be verbal abuse now could turn into physical abuse down the road. No form of abuse is acceptable!

Contrary to what you may believe, *you are not powerless*! You are a worthwhile person and you do not have to continue to accept the mistreatment of your husband. You have the power to make your own choices.

For more information on how to break the cycle of violence in your life
order the complete booklet entitled, A Way of Hope at 1-800-FL-TODAY,
at www.familylife.com, or visit the FamilyLife Resource Center onsite.

Appendix C

Projects for Remarried Couples

The following sections contain projects for couples who are remarried or who are considering remarriage. We know that remarried couples face unique situations and challenges, both in their relationships with each other as well as their children and their stepchildren. For specific application for each project, complete the *Take It Home* pages at the end of the projects in the message section of this manual.

We hope these projects help you practically apply the message of this conference and bring oneness to your blended marriage/family.

APPENDIX
C

Five Threats to Oneness

Remarried Application Project for Sessions 1 and 2

This application project has two sections: the individual section and the interaction section. Be sure to leave adequate time to interact as a couple on the interaction section.

Individual Section

10 Minutes

Setting: Stay together as a couple, but complete this section quickly without any interaction.

Objective: To gain insight into how much the Five Threats have affected your previous marriage(s) and your present marriage

Instructions: All marriages are influenced by the threats to oneness. As you sat through the messages this evening, you undoubtedly reflected on how these threats affected you in your previous marriage(s). In the chart below, rate the effect each of the threats had on your previous marriage(s). Circle any threat that you believe may have been a factor in the break-up of that marriage.

THREATS	HOW MUCH EFFECT			RESULTS IN MY MARRIAGE CAUSED BY THIS THREAT
	LITTLE	SOME	SIGNIFICANT	
1. Difficult adjustments	☐	☐	☐	
2. World's 50/50 pattern	☐	☐	☐	
3. Selfishness	☐	☐	☐	
4. Difficulties, trials, and problems	☐	☐	☐	
5. Extramarital "affairs"	☐	☐	☐	

1. Have you taken responsibility for the part you played in the breakup of your previous marriage(s)? Do you have realistic expectations for your spouse?

2. Now, consider how these same threats are a factor in your present marriage. Note any similarities or patterns that may be re-emerging.

 # Interaction Section

20-30 Minutes

Setting: Stay together for interaction. Find a place where you are able to talk freely.

Objective: To share and gain insight on how your marriage has been affected by these threats

Instructions:

1. Review how the Five Threats to Oneness affected your previous marriage(s) and your present marriage. Be considerate and teachable.

2. Discuss the ways you had hoped your present marriage would be different from your previous marriage. As you look back now, were some of those expectations unrealistic? Which ones?

3. Many remarried couples are surprised by the difficult adjustments they face in a new marriage. You're not alone. Christian author Norm Wright has said that in a first marriage, the "adjustment" phase can take five to seven years. In a remarriage, he says, it takes eight to ten years. Share what has been your most difficult adjustment in your marriage so far. (Don't try to problem-solve now. Just acknowledge the difficulties as you understand them.)

4. Agree on one or two specific action points to protect yourselves against the threats that are most dangerous to your marriage.

5. On the *Take It Home* page, check at least one item that you will do individually or as a couple.

6. Record that action point on the *Take It Home Summary* flap attached to the back cover.

God's Purposes and Plan for Marriage

Remarried Application Project for Sessions 3&4

This application project has two sections: the individual section and the interaction section. Be sure to leave adequate time to interact as a couple on the interaction section.

Individual Section

25 Minutes

Setting: Find a place to be alone, but near your spouse, to complete this section.

Objective: To surface and identify your true feelings toward each other.

Instructions: Spend time in prayer individually in Part One and then complete Part Two.

Part One: (10 Minutes) Spend time in prayer.

1. Confess to God any rejection of, withdrawal from, or bitterness toward your spouse as sin. Thank God for His forgiveness and the cleansing blood of Christ.

> *If we confess our sins, He is faithful and righteous to forgive us our sins and to cleanse us from all unrighteousness.*
>
> 1 John 1:9

2. Remarried couples may hesitate to express total, unconditional commitment to one another because of failures in the past or the death of a spouse. For a marriage to work, you must, by faith, commit to receive your spouse as God's provision for you. This commitment is based on the integrity and sovereignty of God. As you write your love letter, be sure to express your unconditional commitment to your spouse.

3. Commit to God to trust Him with your spouse's differences and weaknesses and to love your spouse unconditionally with Christ's love (apart from performance). Be certain you put this commitment in your love letter.

4. Remarrieds face many distractions and demands that keep them from making their marriage their first priority. Former spouses, children from a previous marriage, finances, and in-laws can easily cause pressure in a marriage that will lead to isolation. Our wedding vows include the phrase "forsaking all others" to remind us that our relationship with our spouse must come before any other relationship (except for our relationship with God). Commit to God that you will make your marriage relationship second only to Christ—even above your children—and express that commitment in your love letter.

APPENDIX
C

Part Two: (15 Minutes)

Write out the answers to the following questions in the form of a love letter. Use the blank Love Letter page (pages 64-65) for your letter.

1. What were the qualities that attracted me the most to you when we first met?

2. What qualities do I appreciate or have I learned to appreciate most about you since we have been married?

3. How have your differences helped me grow spiritually and emotionally?

Interaction Section

15 Minutes

Setting: Get together with your spouse and complete this section. Make sure you can talk freely.

Objective: To share your feelings and commitment with each other

Instructions: Read each question and spend time sharing.

1. Share and discuss your letter.

2. Verbalize to your spouse the commitment you made to God during your individual prayer time.

3. Close your time together by taking turns thanking God for each other.

4. Write the points of action you will take individually, as a couple, and with others on the *Take It Home* page.

5. Then, record that point of action you most want to apply on the *Take It Home Summary* flap attached to the back cover.

Preparation for Marriage:
Engaged Couples
(one or both have been previously married)
Remarried Application Project for Session 5

This application project has two sections: the individual section and the interaction section. Be sure to leave adequate time to interact as a couple on the interaction section.

 ## Individual Section
No Time Limit

Setting: Stay together and complete this section. For fun, keep the results of this section and review them after one year of marriage.

Objective: To find out how well you know each other and to galvanize your commitment to one another

Instructions: Without interaction, complete the chart below. Put an X on

Disciplined	1	2	3	4	5	6	7	8	9	10	Impulsive
Stubborn	1	2	3	4	5	6	7	8	9	10	Humble
Aggressive/Assertive	1	2	3	4	5	6	7	8	9	10	Compliant/Passive
Infatuated Love	1	2	3	4	5	6	7	8	9	10	Realistic Love
Task-Oriented	1	2	3	4	5	6	7	8	9	10	People-Oriented
Center of God's Will	1	2	3	4	5	6	7	8	9	10	Out of God's Will
Pessimistic	1	2	3	4	5	6	7	8	9	10	Optimistic
Outgoing	1	2	3	4	5	6	7	8	9	10	Withdrawn
Forgiving	1	2	3	4	5	6	7	8	9	10	Holds a grudge
High Expectations About Remarriage	1	2	3	4	5	6	7	8	9	10	Low Expectations About Remarriage
Sympathetic	1	2	3	4	5	6	7	8	9	10	Insensitive
Decisive	1	2	3	4	5	6	7	8	9	10	Indecisive
Tense	1	2	3	4	5	6	7	8	9	10	Relaxed
Spendthrift	1	2	3	4	5	6	7	8	9	10	Scrooge
Emotionally Open	1	2	3	4	5	6	7	8	9	10	Emotionally Closed
Good Self-Image	1	2	3	4	5	6	7	8	9	10	Poor Self-Image
Critical	1	2	3	4	5	6	7	8	9	10	Gracious
Growing Spiritually	1	2	3	4	5	6	7	8	9	10	Spiritually Stagnant
Heart for God	1	2	3	4	5	6	7	8	9	10	Lukewarm to God
Idealistic	1	2	3	4	5	6	7	8	9	10	Realistic
Openly Affectionate	1	2	3	4	5	6	7	8	9	10	Reserved With Affection

the number that best describes you on each quality or trait. Circle the number that best describes your fiancé/fiancée. Be truthful. When both are finished, discuss your answers.

Interaction Section

No Time Limit

Setting: This is the time for serious, personal reflection on the insights you gained from the individual section. This is to be done in complete privacy.

Objective: To seriously evaluate your relationship in terms of how well you, as a couple, are suited for remarriage

1. Does the individual section cause you to question God's leading toward remarriage?   Yes   No   If yes, why?

2. Are you willing to receive this person with all of his strengths and weaknesses as God's personal provision for your needs?

3. Identify any issues from either's past relationships that could become a stumbling block in your future marriage.

4. Jot down any parental or stepparental expectations that you have of one another. (Be specific regarding roles as nurturer, disciplinarian, and spiritual teacher.)

5. What action steps should you take in light of your answers to questions 1, 2, 3, and 4?

6. On the Points of Action page, write one point of action that you will take individually, as a couple, or with others.

7. Then, record that point of action on the Key Points of Action flap attached to the back cover.

8. Schedule a time to complete the post-conference project on the next page as a way for confirming God's will for your relationship.

9. Very important: Schedule your one-year, 10,000 mile marriage tune-up for the next Weekend to Remember Conference. We promise you will hear more the next time.

Preparation for Marriage:
Pre-engaged Couples
(one or both have been previously married)
Remarried Application Project for Session 5

This application project has two sections: the individual section and the interaction section. Be sure to leave adequate time to interact as a couple on the interaction section.

Individual Section
Post Conference

Setting: This project should be done completely alone. Schedule a private place, away from distractions, where you can pray, study God's Word, think, and work without interruption. It is imperative that you spend this time away from each other.

Objective: To discern God's will for marriage

Instructions:

1. Schedule two days, probably a weekend. Be sure to include at least one night to "sleep on your decision."
2. Spend time with God in prayer and reading His Word. The Psalms and Proverbs are great to help prepare your heart.
3. Review your Weekend to Remember Conference notebook. Special review should be given to the messages "God's Purposes for Oneness" and "God's Plan for Oneness."
4. Use this checklist to remember to take the following:

   - ❑ Bible, notebook, and pen
   - ❑ Weekend to Remember Conference notebook
   - ❑ A prayerful heart
   - ❑ Audio series: "Are You Ready? Becoming Mr. or Mrs. Right" FamilyLife Product #790

Part One

Pray and work your way through these six steps from the conference message on God's will. Then complete the seventh step.

Step 1: Are you right with God? Confess your sins and humble yourself before God. Relinquish all rights to your life to God. Read Romans 12:1-2 and Psalm 90:11-12.

If I regard wickedness in my heart, the Lord will not hear.

Psalm 66:18

Step 2: Write down 10 reasons you think your fiancé/fiancée is the one you should marry.

1.

2.

3.

4.

5.

6.

7.

8.

9.

10.

Step 3: Write 10 reasons this is the time in your life that you should marry.

1.

2.

3.

4.

5.

6.

7.

8.

9.

10.

Step 4: Answer the following questions:

    a. Do you both have a heart for God?

    b. Is Jesus Christ at the center of your relationship?

    c. Are you both pursuing God?

    d. Are your philosophies compatible?

    e. Are your goals and plans for the future compatible?

    f. Can you accept your personality differences?

    g. Are you emotionally compatible? Are there presently any areas of your emotional relationship that remain uncomfortable, difficult to discuss, or that cause regular conflict?

    h. What are others saying about your relationship?

    i. What would be most difficult about ending this relationship right now?

    j. Can you live without this person?

    k. Are you willing to commit yourself to this person unconditionally for the rest of your life?

    l. Have you given yourself and your children ample time (three to five years) to grieve the losses you've experienced?

    m. If you were hurt by your former spouse in your previous marriage, have you forgiven him? (See Matthew 18:21-35.)

    n. Have you been able to forgive your potential spouse's former spouse for what he did? (See Matthew 18:21-35.)

    o. If your potential spouse has children, are you willing to take on the additional role of being a stepparent?

Step 5: Write out a list of your fears.

Step 6: Confess or acknowledge those fears to God. Read 1 John 1:9.

Step 7: Most children consider a parent's remarriage to be yet another loss in their life. If you have children, to what degree have you explored a possible remarriage with them? How might your remarriage bring additional pain to their already wounded heart?

Step 8: Can you commit to God to accept the other as His provision for your   needs? Can you receive that person just as he is right now?

Step 9: Write out the commitment to God. If you cannot receive him as God's provision, then write out a resolution to God that releases your potential spouse from the relationship.

Step 10: Hold your decision privately for 24 hours, allowing God to confirm it with His conviction that you are to marry. Continue to pray during this time, allowing God to give you freedom to move forward. Do not move forward in the relationship without God's peace!

Step 11: Seek out a stepfamily support group or start reading a Christ-centered book on stepfamily life. Start learning all you can about how to make your stepfamily successful.

Part Two

Make your decision known as you complete steps eight and nine from the conference message on God's purposes.

Step 1: Tell one close friend, which allows him to confirm your decision and to hold you accountable. It is very important that you continue to be accountable to a friend after you make your decision. After you have verbalized your decision (step eight) do not back down on your commitment without first discussing it with your friend.

Step 2: Verbalize your decision to your potential spouse.

Part Three

Very important. Schedule your one-year, 10,000 mile marriage tune-up for the next Weekend to Remember conference. We promise you will hear more the next time.

Step 1: Write one point of action you will take immediately, as a couple, or with others on the *Take It Home* page at the end of Session 5.

Step 2: Then, record that *Take It Home* action onto the *Take It Home Summary* flap attached to the back cover.

APPENDIX

C

Sexual Intimacy: Expression of Oneness

Remarried Application Project for Session 8

This application project has two sections: the individual section and the interaction section. Be sure to leave adequate time to interact as a couple on the interaction section.

Individual Section

25 Minutes

Setting: Stay together as a couple, but complete this section quickly without any interaction.

Objective: To open up communication by surfacing and identifying personal feelings, attitudes, and thoughts you have on this subject

Instructions: Complete this section individually.

Part One:

How satisfied are you with the way you and your spouse handle the following aspects of your sexual relationship? Circle the number that corresponds to your answer. Underline the answer you think your spouse will select.

LOW SATISFACTION					HIGH SATISFACTION	
1	2	3	4	5		The quality of our companionship
1	2	3	4	5		The level of our commitment
1	2	3	4	5		The fire of our passion
1	2	3	4	5		The depth of our spiritual intimacy
1	2	3	4	5		Viewing sex with positive anticipation
1	2	3	4	5		The way we decide to have sex together
1	2	3	4	5		The amount of communication during lovemaking (such as discussing better ways of pleasing each other)
1	2	3	4	5		The frequency of our physical intimacy
1	2	3	4	5		Gentleness and tenderness during lovemaking
1	2	3	4	5		The variety of our sexual experiences together
1	2	3	4	5		The selflessness displayed in our lovemaking
1	2	3	4	5		The understanding I have of my spouse in this area
1	2	3	4	5		The overall temperature of our love for one another

APPENDIX C

Part Two:

Answer the following questions.

1. List any fears you may have about sex. How can your spouse alleviate these fears?

2. Do you fully trust your spouse with your body? If not, in what aspect? Why? Refer to 1 Corinthians 7:3-5.

3. List any incorrect attitudes you may have about your body or your spouse's body. Refer to Song of Solomon 5:1-16 and 7:1-9.

APPENDIX
C

4. How has your previous marriage affected your sexual desire for your spouse?

5. In what ways are you concerned about your spouse's previous sexual relationships?

6. Depending upon the age of your children/stepchildren, demonstrating affection to one another can be awkward. Furthermore, a "locked bedroom door" can draw attention to your sexuality. What fears or concerns do you have about this common struggle?

7. How will you manage the sexual boundaries that must exist between stepfathers and stepdaughters or between stepsiblings?

Part Three:

Complete the following:

1. In leading up to physical love, I like for you to ...

2. When we are sharing physical love, I like for you to ...

3. I feel discouraged when you ...

4. I am most drawn to you sexually when you ...

Part Four:

1. Look back over parts one through three and note what changes in your own behavior could make improvements in your physical relationship.

2. In prayer, confess any resentment and bitterness you may have.

3. Recognize that sex is a gift from God and that an attitude of giving establishes oneness.

4. Agree together that your sexual union is a reflection of your intimacy and union with one another and with God in Jesus Christ.

Interaction Section
30 Minutes

Setting: Stay together as a couple and complete this section.

Objective: To discuss the feelings, attitudes, and thoughts that each of you have on this subject

Instructions:

1. Share and discuss as a couple the work you completed in parts one through four. Be sure to interact with an attitude of understanding, sympathy, and forgiveness.

APPENDIX

C

2. Schedule a whole day and night within the next month when both of you can get away for a special time of communication and intimacy.

3. Pray together and thank God for each other as His provision. Make a commitment to each other to improve communication and intimacy.

4. Write the points of action you will take individually, as a couple, and with others on the *Take It Home* page.

5. Then, record that point of action you most want to apply on the *Take It Home Summary* flap attached to the back cover.

The Wife's Responsibility for Oneness/Mom

Remarried Application Project for Sessions 10&11

This application project has two sections: the individual section and the interaction section. Be sure to leave adequate time to interact as a couple on the interaction section.

Individual Section

35 Minutes

Setting: Find a place to be alone and complete this section.
Objective: To discover needs that you and your spouse have.
Instructions: Complete both parts as instructed.

APPENDIX C

Part One:

1. Rate the statements on the chart below from 1 to 5.

STRONGLY DISAGREE		STRONGLY AGREE	
1 2 3 4 5		The world's plan has distracted me from my responsibilities as a wife and mother.
1 2 3 4 5		My attitudes toward my husband reflect support and confidence in him.
1 2 3 4 5		My attitudes and actions toward my husband show him respect.
1 2 3 4 5		My attitudes and actions toward my husband show him love.
1 2 3 4 5		My attitude towards my husband reflects contentment and trust in God.
1 2 3 4 5		I am growing spiritually.
1 2 3 4 5		I support my husband's responsibility to initiate spiritually in our home.
1 2 3 4 5		I stay available to my husband with adequate time and energy.
1 2 3 4 5		My husband knows I admire him.
1 2 3 4 5		I am a positive encouragement to him.
1 2 3 4 5		I find myself repeating destructive patterns from the past as a wife/mother.
1 2 3 4 5		I am a good friend of his.
1 2 3 4 5		I do not often negatively compare my husband with my previous husband.
1 2 3 4 5		I am willing to follow his direction for our home.
1 2 3 4 5		I accept him regardless of his performance.
1 2 3 4 5		I respect him.

STRONGLY DISAGREE					STRONGLY AGREE	
1	2	3	4	5		I consider him my top priority.
1	2	3	4	5		I always back him up and verbally support him when we are in public.
1	2	3	4	5		I express enjoyment in our sexual life.
1	2	3	4	5		I am spending consistent time in Bible study so I will be biblically accurate in my responsibilities as a wife and mother.
1	2	3	4	5		I communicate love and admiration for my husband in front of our children and/or my stepchildren.
1	2	3	4	5		Biblical priorities are more important to me than status and lifestyle.
1	2	3	4	5		I save time and energy to nurture my children and/or my stepchildren.
1	2	3	4	5		I model the character I want my children and/or my stepchildren to emulate.
1	2	3	4	5		My home is a top priority.
1	2	3	4	5		I am allowing my stepchildren to set the pace for my relationship with them (regarding closeness and their willingness to receive discipline from me).
1	2	3	4	5		I do not allow myself to compete with my stepchildren for their father's attention.
1	2	3	4	5		I do my part to help my stepchildren have regular access to their biological mother and extended family.
1	2	3	4	5		I understand that stepmothers are often taken for granted by their stepchildren; my source of strength comes from the Lord.
1	2	3	4	5		When I have complaints about my husband's children, I work hard to express them to my husband in a reasonable manner—not being overly critical.
1	2	3	4	5		I am continually being intentional in building a relationship with my stepchildren.

APPENDIX

C

Part Two:

Answer the following questions.

1. What do you think your husband's five greatest needs are? How can you begin to meet them practically?

2. What are your own five greatest needs as a wife and mother? How can your husband help provide leadership for you in these areas?

3. What makes each of your children and/or stepchildren unique? List the two greatest needs of each child.

4. In what ways are you confused about your roles as wife, mother, and/or stepmother?

Part Three:

Complete the following worksheet.

WIFE'S RESPONSIBILITY	List one action point that will help you improve in each area.
Love	
Support	
Respect	

MOM	
Home builder	
Lover of children	
Teacher of children	

Interaction Section

No Time Limit

Setting: Find a time to meet with your husband after you both have finished the individual section.

Objective: To raise your awareness of each other's needs

Instructions:

1. Discuss your work on parts one and two of the individual sections.

2. Listen to him as he shares his part.

3. Write one point of action you will take individually, as a couple, or with others on the *Take It Home* page.

4. Then, record that action point onto the *Take It Home Summary* flap on the back cover.

The Husband's Responsibility for Oneness/Dad

Remarried Application Project for Sessions 10&11

This application project has two sections: the individual section and the interaction section. Be sure to leave adequate time to interact as a couple on the interaction section.

Individual Section

35 Minutes

Setting: Find a place to be alone and complete this section.
Objective: To discover needs you, your spouse, and your children have.
Instructions: Complete both parts as instructed.

Part One

1. Rate the statements on the chart below from 1 to 5.

STRONGLY DISAGREE					STRONGLY AGREE	Statement
1	2	3	4	5		The world's plan has distracted me from my responsibilities as a husband and father.
1	2	3	4	5		My leadership style makes biblical submission easy and reasonable for my wife.
1	2	3	4	5		My leadership style makes my wife feel cherished and understood.
1	2	3	4	5		My leadership is characterized by taking the initiative.
1	2	3	4	5		My leadership style allows our home to be well-managed.
1	2	3	4	5		I verbalize acceptance and honor to my wife.
1	2	3	4	5		I show love for my wife with sacrificial action.
1	2	3	4	5		I demonstrate love even when I don't feel it.
1	2	3	4	5		I know my wife's needs.
1	2	3	4	5		I esteem my wife in her role as a wife (and mother).
1	2	3	4	5		I live with my wife in an understanding way.
1	2	3	4	5		I am growing spiritually.
1	2	3	4	5		My wife knows she is my top priority.
1	2	3	4	5		I find myself repeating destructive patterns from the past as a husband/father.
1	2	3	4	5		I do not often negatively compare my wife with my previous wife.
1	2	3	4	5		My wife knows that I need her.

APPENDIX C

STRONGLY DISAGREE					STRONGLY AGREE	
1	2	3	4	5		I initiate spiritual guidance to my children and/or stepchilden.
1	2	3	4	5		I model the character I want my children and/or stepchilden to emulate.
1	2	3	4	5		I use daily opportunities to equip and train my children and/or stepchilden.
1	2	3	4	5		I am aware of the unique personality needs of each of my children and/or stepchilden.
1	2	3	4	5		I encourage my stepchildren to respect and honor their biological father.
1	2	3	4	5		I am allowing my stepchildren to set the pace for my relationship with them (regarding closeness and their willingness to receive discipline from me).
1	2	3	4	5		I do not allow myself to compete with my stepchildren for their mother's attention.
1	2	3	4	5		I do my part to help my stepchildren have regular access to their biological father and extended family.
1	2	3	4	5		I understand that stepfathers are often taken for granted by their stepchildren; my source of strength comes from the Lord.
1	2	3	4	5		When I have complaints about my wife's children, I work hard to express them to my wife in a reasonable manner—not being overly critical.
1	2	3	4	5		I am continually being intentional in building a relationship with my stepchildren.
1	2	3	4	5		I am able to find ways to lead my stepchildren (perhaps differently than my own children).
1	2	3	4	5		I respect and empower my wife's role with her children and do not try to dictate their relationship. I lead by modeling a spiritual course for our home.
1	2	3	4	5		I am spending consistent time studying the Bible so our family remains biblically accurate.

2. Underline any of the statements from the previous chart that you feel needs urgent change.

Part Two

Answer the following questions.

1. What do you think are your wife's five greatest needs? How can you practically begin to meet them?

2. What are your own five greatest needs as a husband and father? How can your wife be a "helper" to you?

3. What makes each of your children and/or stepchildren unique? List the two greatest needs of each child.

4. In what ways are you confused about your roles as husband, father, and/or stepfather?

Part Three

Complete the following worksheet.

HUSBAND'S RESPONSIBILITY	List one action point that will help you improve in each area.
Love	
Lead	

DAD	List one action point that will help you improve in each area.
Manager	
Minister	
Model	

Interaction Section

No Time Limit

Setting: Find a time to meet with your wife after you both have finished the individual sections

Objective: To raise your awareness of each other's needs.
Instructions:

1. Discuss your work on parts one and two of the individual sections.

2. Listen to her as she shares her part.

3. Write one point of action you will take individually, as a couple, or with others on the *Take It Home* page.

4. Then, record that action point onto the *Take It Home Summary* flap attached to the back cover.

Resolving Conflict

Remarried Application Project for Session 12

This application project has two sections: the individual section and the interaction section. Be sure to leave adequate time to interact as a couple on the interaction section.

Individual Section

25 Minutes

Setting: Stay together as a couple, but complete this section quickly without any interaction.

Objective: To begin the process of practicing forgiveness

Instructions: Complete both parts of this section.

Part One

It's critical for married couples to understand their pattern for resolving conflict and to adopt a biblical pattern. Before moving on to Part Two, ask yourself these questions:

1. What was your pattern of resolving conflict in your previous marriage(s)?

2. How has that pattern continued in your current marriage? Has this benefited or damaged your relationship with your spouse?

3. How do you respond when you are hurt? Are you a "stuffer" or a "blower"?

4. Do you struggle with admitting your failures with your spouse?

5. Is it difficult for you to grant forgiveness?

Warning: As you begin to practice seeking and granting forgiveness in the remainder of this project, you may feel the need to address forgiveness issues from a previous marriage or relationship. If so, jot these concerns down as they come to your mind, but give attention to them later. For now, focus on your current marriage and the issues at hand.

Also, do not overlook the significance of forgiving people in your past as a way of generating intimacy in the present. Pray that God will grant you the strength and perseverance to avoid habits and patterns from the past.

Part Two

Prepare your heart by humbling yourself before God. Confess any anger that may keep "the wall" up and your spouse at a distance. Thank God that He has forgiven you (read 1 John 1:8-9). Then, acknowledge your willingness before God to seek forgiveness from your spouse. Likewise, prepare your heart to grant forgiveness to your spouse by thanking God for him.

Therefore, confess your sins to one another, and pray for one another, so that you may be healed. The effective prayer of a righteous man can accomplish much.

James 5:16

Interaction Section
20-30 Minutes

Setting: Stay together for interaction.

1. Make sure you are able to talk freely.

2. Don't be defensive. Acknowledge your contribution to problems.

3. Concentrate on using "I" statements only. Avoid words like "if," "but," and "maybe."

4. Seek to listen.

5. Express the truth in love.

6. Be willing to make concessions to reach agreement.

Objective: To verbally seek or grant forgiveness with your spouse.

Instructions:

Step 1

1. Husband:

    a. Share with your wife the answers listed in Part One of the Individual Section.

    b. While looking at your wife, restate the offense that you would like to seek forgiveness for, and ask her forgiveness.

2. Wife:

    a. Grant forgiveness to your husband with your words. Be honest.

    b. Then, by deed, take the offense written down on the piece of paper and throw it away or burn it as a symbolic gesture of the freedom forgiveness grants.

Step 2

1. Wife:

    a. Share with your husband the answers listed in Part One of the Individual Section.

    b. While looking at your husband, restate the offense that you would like to seek forgiveness for.

2. Husband:

    a. Grant forgiveness to your wife with your words. Be honest.

    b. Then, by deed, take the offense written down on the piece of paper and throw it away or burn it as a symbolic gesture of the freedom forgiveness grants.

Step 3

Write one point of action you will take individually, as a couple, or with others on the *Take It Home* page.

Step 4

Then, record that point of action onto the *Take It Home Summary* flap attached to the back cover.

Bonus Project

No time limit

Many remarried couples struggle in their current marriage because of unresolved hurt and anger from their previous marriage. Our goal here should be to obey Romans 12:18: "If possible, so far as it depends on you, be at peace with all men."

Also look at Matthew 18:21-35 and see how important it is to God that we forgive from our hearts. These verses are Jesus' express instructions for freedom from past hurts and offenses. We must always remember that we will not be forgiven unless we forgive.

Matthew 6:14-15 tells us, "For if you forgive others for their transgressions, your heavenly Father will also forgive you. But if you do not forgive others, then your Father will not forgive your transgressions." Yes, it's radical. It's hard. But it's non-negotiable with Jesus. It can only be done by faith in Jesus, taking Him at His Word, and responding in trust and obedience.

Pre-married Project

Because we should seek to honor God in all we do, say, and think, it is very important to be sure that we are acting in accordance with the Lord's will when we marry. Jesus said in Matthew 19:6b, "What therefore God has joined together, let no man separate."

If your previous spouse is alive and unmarried, we encourage you to seek the advice of your pastor before you decide to remarry. Ask your pastor to discuss with you the passages in Matthew 5:31-32 and 19:1-12, Mark 10:1-12, Luke 16:18, and Romans 7:1-3, 1 Corinthians 7:10-40, 2 Corinthians 6:14-18 (as they apply to your particular situation).

Couples who are free to remarry need to have discussed and worked through the relational issues that led to the breakup of their first marriage. For example:

1. How did you resolve conflict in your first marriage?

2. How did you live out your roles?

3. What communication problems were present in your first marriage? Did these problems surface after the wedding, or did you experience them with your first spouse prior to marriage?

4. What habits or addictions were a part of your previous relationship?

5. What steps have you taken to grant or receive forgiveness from God and your ex-spouse?

6. How well do you and your ex-spouse cooperate regarding your children? How might a lack of cooperation hurt a new marriage?

7. Are any harmful patterns from the past showing up again in your present relationship?

Appendix D
Alumni Projects

You have most likely chosen to attend another FamilyLife Conference for several reasons. Perhaps you have come because you want to grow deeper in your marriage and relationship with God. Maybe you have brought some friends, hoping that their marriage will be touched like yours was. Or perhaps you have come for training, because you have a vision for other couples in your church. Whatever the case may be, we know that this weekend can be a powerful experience for you.

In this manual we have gathered material from our various HomeBuilders Couples Series® books and developed special alumni projects just for you. These projects are intended to be optional. At the end of a given session, you and your spouse will be given the opportunity to determine the project that best fits your needs.

The table below may help you with your decision. We hope you will be challenged to apply God's Word to your lives, and in turn, to tell others.

PROJECT NAME	PAGE #	MAIN PROJECT OBJECTIVE	ALUMNI PROJECT OBJECTIVE
Five Threats to Oneness	240	Gain insight into how the five threats to marital oneness have affected your marriage.	Foresee how the five threats may affect your marriage in the future if they are not dealt with.
God's Purpose and Plan for Marriage	242	Surface and identify your true feelings toward each other.	Determine how God's purposes for marriage are displayed in your relationship.
Sexual Intimacy: Expression of Oneness	244	Open up communication by surfacing and identifying feelings, attitudes, and thoughts you have on this subject.	Find ways to develop greater sexual intimacy in your marriage.
The Wife's Responsibility for Oneness/Mom	246	Raise awareness of the needs that you, your spouse, and your children have.	Understand and adapt to your husband.
The Husband's Responsibility for Oneness/Dad	248	Raise awareness of the needs that you, your spouse, and your children have.	Learn to love and build up your wife as you lead.
Resolving Conflict	251	Begin the process of practicing forgiveness.	Recognize areas of conflict in your marriage and understand how your spouse will typically respond when conflict occurs.

Five Threats to Oneness

Alumni Application Project 1

This project has two sections: the individual section and the interaction section. Be sure to leave adequate time to interact as a couple on the interaction section.

Individual Section
15 minutes

Setting: Stay together as a couple but complete this section quickly without any interaction.

Objective: To determine how the five threats may affect your marriage in the future if they are not dealt with.

Instructions: Think about the next five to 20 years of your life. If you do not address the effects of the five threats to your marriage, what do you think will happen to your relationship? Place an asterisk (*) next to the threat that may have the greatest effect.

THREATS	RESULTS IN FIVE TO 20 YEARS
1. Difficult adjustments	
2. World's 50/50 plan	
3. Selfishness	
4. Difficulties, trials, and problems	
5. Extramarital "affairs"	

Instructions: It is a helpful exercise to envision what you'd like your marriage to look like 20 years down the road. What do you want to feel toward each other? What type of relationship do you want to have? Write a brief description of your hopes and dreams.

Interaction Section

20-30 minutes

Setting: Stay together for interaction. Find a place where you are able to talk freely.

Objective: To share and gain insight on how the five threats may affect your marriage in the future

Instructions:

1. Share how you believe the five threats may affect your marriage in the future and why. Remain sensitive to each other. Listen carefully before responding.

2. Share your hopes and dreams for your relationship.

3. Agree on one or two action points to protect yourself against those threats that are most dangerous.

4. Take time to pray together, and ask God's help in building a godly marriage.

God's Purpose and Plan for Marriage

Alumni Application Project 2

This project has two sections: the individual section and the interaction section. Be sure to leave adequate time to interact as a couple on the interaction section.

Individual Section
15 minutes

Setting: Stay together as a couple, but complete this section without interaction.

Objective: To determine how God's purposes for marriage are displayed in your relationship

Instructions: Answer each of the following questions and prepare to discuss them with your spouse.

1. What would your closest friends say is the purpose of your marriage?

2. In which of God's purposes are you succeeding? (Mirroring God's image, mutually completing one another, multiplying a godly legacy.)

3. Which ones need work in your marriage? In what way?

4. What hinders your success in accomplishing these purposes?

5. What one step could you take this week to move toward fulfilling one of God's purposes in your marriage?

Interaction Section
15 minutes

Setting: Get together with your spouse and complete this section.

Objective: To determine how your marriage may better reflect God's purposes

Instructions: Compare answers to the questions in the individual section. Then, take time to pray together and identify one or two steps that you may take in your marriage to improve how you live out God's purposes for your relationship.

APPENDIX
D

1.

2.

Sexual Intimacy: Expression of Oneness

Alumni Application Project 3

This project has two sections: the individual section and the interaction section. Be sure to leave adequate time to interact as a couple on the interaction section.

Individual Section
20 minutes

Setting: Stay together as a couple but complete this section quickly, without any interaction.

Objective: To find ways to develop greater sexual intimacy in your marriage

Instructions: Complete this section, and prepare to share your insights with your spouse.

1. What would your spouse say are the primary activities that rob the two of you of time to nurture intimacy? Check appropriate boxes.

   ❑ Watching TV   ❑ Hobbies, sports, or recreation activities

   ❑ Reading   ❑ Church activities

   ❑ Children   ❑ Civic activities

   ❑ Work   ❑ Other_____

2. Husband—many women express a need for their husbands to share more of their lives with them. What are some practical ways you can work at being more open and transparent with your wife and share more of your life with her?

   Why do you think openness and transparency are important to a woman in regard to intimacy?

3. Wife—Ephesians 5:33 says, "Nevertheless, let each individual among you also love his own wife even as himself; and let the wife see to it that she respect her husband." What are some practical things you can do to give your husband respect as a man?

How do you think that your husband's need for respect relates to sexual intimacy?

 # Interaction Section

20-30 minutes

Setting: Stay together as a couple in a place where you are able to share openly.

Objective: To discuss ways in which intimacy may be cultivated in your marriage

Instructions:

1. Share your insights and answers from the individual section. Husbands, respond to your wife's thoughts about your need for respect. Wives, talk about how the power of openness and transparency affects you in your marital relationship. Write down your insights and action points.

2. As we have learned, non-sexual physical affection is one of the most powerful relationship-builders for a woman. And yet, this same affection can quickly arouse a man to desire sexual intercourse. Together, talk about this and determine some ways in which "safe touching" and affection may occur without the husband feeling frustration and rejection, or the wife feeling pressure to perform sexually. Discuss how you will communicate with your spouse when you begin to experience these feelings.

3. End this project by praying together and thanking God for your spouse. Ask the Lord to help you be more sensitive to your spouse's needs, and accepting of his differences.

The Wife's Responsibility for Oneness

Alumni Application Project 4

This project has two sections: the individual section and the interaction section. Be sure to leave adequate time to interact as a couple on the interaction section.

Individual Section
35 minutes

Setting: Find a place to be near your husband, and complete this section.

Objective: To help you better understand and adapt to your husband

Instructions: Which of the following attitudes are the most difficult for you to demonstrate toward your husband? (Check the ones that apply.)

APPENDIX D

❑ Understanding his manhood _____

❑ Understanding his need for work _____

❑ Understanding his sexual need _____

❑ Giving him respect _____

❑ Adapting to him _____

❑ Sharing his dreams _____

Next to each attitude that you checked above, tell why you struggle in that area. What can you do about this problem area? Pray? Change your focus? Something else?

What are your husband's dreams and goals? List as many as you can think of.

1. _____

2. _____

3. _____

4. _____

5. _____

6. _____

How can you best encourage him to achieve these goals?

3. Are you willing for him to become and do all God has planned? What do you fear the most? A move (near or far)? A change in your finances? A change in your job? Or the role you would be expected to fill as a result of your husband's position? Write down how you feel.

In prayer, give that area of fear and insecurity to God. Ask Him to free you from that personal concern so you will not be a hindrance to God's plan for your husband's life, but a true biblical helper.

4. What are your husband's positive character qualities? Is he compassionate, kind, and sensitive toward people? Is he disciplined and dedicated? Is he faithful and loyal, persevering in difficulties? Do the words "truthful," "honest," or "decisive" describe your spouse? What are his talents and strengths? Make a list. Refresh your memory. Refurbish your respect.

APPENDIX

D

 # Interaction Section
No Time Limit

Setting: Stay together in a place so that you may share openly with one another.

Objective: To share what you think regarding your husband's personal characteristics, hopes, and dreams, and identify how you see yourself supporting him.

Instructions: Interact as a couple.

1. Share with your husband what you admire and respect about him.

2. Share with your husband the list you made of his dreams and goals. Circle the ones he indicates he feels strongly about. How "right on target" are you? Assure him that you want to share those dreams and work toward those goals with him.

The Husband's Responsibility for Oneness

Alumni Application Project 5

This project has two sections: the individual section and the interaction section. Be sure to leave adequate time to interact as a couple on the interaction section.

Individual Section

35 minutes

Setting: Stay close as a couple, and complete this section.

Objective: To help you learn to love and build up your wife as you lead her

Instructions: The following questions will help you "inventory" your most valuable friend: your wife. By making yourself answer these questions periodically, you become better able to protect her and lead her with understanding.

1. What is the pace of her life?

2. Does your schedule cause her more problems than it does you? How does it affect her?

3. Does your schedule allow for any breathers for her? For you? What do you need to do differently?

4. What kind of pace can she keep? For how long?

5. What does she need after an intensely busy or difficult period of time?

6. What tends to crush her? What deflates her?

7. What causes her to feel she is failing? What can you do about it?

8. What decisions do you need to make that will reduce pressure or break up a logjam?

9. Are you putting off some things that, if you did them, would facilitate her daily routine and thereby help her in the long run? If so, what?

10. What directions can you give to protect her as she moves through a difficult period of time?

11. Does she need to be rescued for an evening? A weekend? An extended period? What should the agenda be for your time?

12. When can you carry her off for a romantic retreat just for the two of you? How can you surprise her?

Close by praying for your wife. Ask God to show you what it truly means to love her even as He loves us.

Husband, love your wives, just as Christ also loved the church and gave Himself up for her; that He might sanctify her, having cleansed her by the washing of water with the word, that He might present to Himself the church in all her glory, having no spot or wrinkle or any such thing; but that she should be holy and blameless. So husbands ought also to love their own wives as their own bodies. He who loves his own wife loves himself; for no one ever hated his own flesh, but nourishes and cherishes it, just as Christ also does the church, because we are members of His body. For this cause a man shall leave his father and mother, and shall cleave to his wife; and the two shall become one flesh. This mystery is great; but I am speaking with reference to Christ and the church. Nevertheless let each individual among you also love his own wife even as himself; and let the wife see to it that she respect her husband.

Ephesians 5:25-33

Interaction Section

No Time Limit

APPENDIX

D

Setting: Stay together in a place so that you may share openly with one another.

Objective: To share how you may serve your wife as you lead and care for her.

Instructions:

1. Share your answers to the first five questions, then ask your wife to answer the same questions; listen carefully.

2. Pray together. Ask God to help you be a good steward of your wife. Thank Him for the opportunity He has entrusted you with to lead her.

Resolving Conflict

Alumni Application Project 6

This project has two sections: the individual section and the interaction section. Be sure to leave adequate time to interact as a couple on the interaction section.

Individual Section
25 minutes

Setting: Stay together as a couple but complete this section quickly, without any interaction.

Objective: To help you recognize areas of conflict in your marriage, and to understand how your spouse typically will respond when conflict occurs.

Instructions:

1. What do you think are some common sources of conflict in your relationship?

   a. _____

   _____

   b. _____

   _____

   c. _____

   _____

   d. _____

   _____

   e. _____

   _____

2. Many people withdraw from conflict; others pursue it. Which do you do and why? How does your spouse respond?

3. Following a conflict, how are you typically affected? Are you angry, quiet, stubborn, sad, talkative, repentant ... ?

4. If you have children, how does conflict between you and your spouse affect them?

5. As you look at how you and your spouse relate to each other, how would you rate your effectiveness in handling conflict? Circle the number you think most applies to your marriage:

1	2	3	4	5
ineffective				very effective

6. If you could change one thing about how you and your spouse handle conflict, what would it be?

APPENDIX

D

Interaction Section

20-30 minutes

Setting: Stay together as a couple in a place where you may share openly with one another.

Objective: To gain understanding and to find better ways to resolve conflict in your marriage

Instructions:

1. Share and discuss the questions you answered during your individual time.

2. List three things you can start doing now to improve how you handle conflict as a couple.

3. Commit yourselves to putting these three ideas into action during your next conflict.

4. Take time to ask for each other's forgiveness if necessary. Pray for God's guidance.

Will you join FamilyLife in the battle for strong families?

Did you know that many people who attend a FamilyLife Conference receive some form of scholarship from other people? These are single parents, inner-city couples, pastors, and people all across the country in need of God's blueprints for the family. Many of them are on the brink of divorce. Will you help us reach more people who need to experience God's life-changing power in their lives?

Here Is Where I Want My Gift to Help:
❒ Conference scholarship fund (1994105)
❒ Area of greatest need for FamilyLife (2294554)

Here Is How I Want to Help:
❒ I want to give to FamilyLife. By giving, I become a FamilyLife Champion. I am enclosing a special gift of:
❒ $50   ❒ $100   ❒ $250   ❒ $ _____

You may also become a FamilyLife Champion by calling us at 1-800-FL-TODAY, 24 hours a day (1-800-358-6329), or by visiting www.familylife.com to make a donation.

Name _____

Address _____

City _____ State _____ ZIP code _____

Phone (H) _____ (W) _____

E-mail _____

Please make checks payable to FamilyLife. Thank you! Your gift is tax deductible as allowed by law. Return to: FamilyLife, P. O. Box 7111, Little Rock, AR 72223-7111.

FamilyLife, a division of Campus Crusade for Christ International, is a charter member of the Evangelical Council for Financial Accountability. This, along with up-to-date accounting procedures and a commitment to remain debt free in our operating budget, helps to ensure the highest level of integrity. More specific financial information is available upon request.

FamilyLife relies on the support of friends like you. It is never our intention to cause feelings of pressure or obligation for financial partnership. Our friends are invited to join us as partners in this effort only as they feel led by God to do so. We depend wholly on Him to speak to His people about our ministry needs and opportunities, and pray that our friends will respond only by His leading.

CHARTER
ECFA
MEMBER

A higher standard.
A higher purpose.

FLCONF

Conference Sessions Answer Guide

**FIVE THREATS
TO ONENESS**
(Sessions 1 and 2)
culture
backgrounds
motivations
expectations
performance
self-destruct
self-centered
selfishness
reality
romance
anticipate
respond properly
response
escape
search

**GOD'S PURPOSES
FOR ONENESS**
(Session 3)
commitment
first
interdependent
priority
oneness
agreement
together
Creator
companionship
together
each other
ambassadors
context
multiply
team
children
Satan
independence
middle
attacks

**GOD'S PLAN FOR
ONENESS**
(Session 4)
alone
need
provided
receive
choose to
character
goodness
differences
hindrances
tools
weaknesses
justification

self-centeredness
admit
placing
receive
transparency
sacrificial

**PREPARATION FOR
MARRIAGE**
(Session 5)
(no blanks to complete)

**GOD'S POWER FOR
ONENESS**
(Session 6)
relationship
separated
died
rose
only
receive
forgiven
eternal
Holy Spirit
God
teaches
convicts
unhindered
desire
confess
surrender

**UNDERSTANDING
COMMUNICATION I**
(Session 7)
value
care
fakes
threatening
attitude
priority
acceptance
enemy
God
freedom
pattern
self-image
pride
hesitant
angry
risk
God
spouse
God's Word
friendships
opportunities
principles

**SEXUAL INTIMACY—
COMMUNICATION II**
(Session 8)
God's
process
pleasure
companionship
commitment
passion
spiritual intimacy
physical
mental
emotional
spiritual
depth
risky
routine
shallow

**ENGAGEMENT—
PREPARATION
FOR ONENESS**
(Session 9)
(no blanks to complete)

**THE WIFE'S
RESPONSIBILITY
FOR ONENESS**
(Session 10)
discernment
equal value
interdependent
head
helper
worth
worth
failures
action
priority
time
responsiveness
complementary
job
public
home
submission
encouraging
assisting
praying
voluntarily
understanding
appreciation
encouragement
admiration
right
attitude
decision

MOM
(Session 11)
powerful
irreplaceable
impossible
calling
culture
call
primary
reflects
spiritual
needs
wants
appropriate
undermined
attitude
nurturing
time
training
primary

**THE HUSBAND'S
RESPONSIBILITY
FOR ONENESS**
(Session 10)
order
head
helper
interdependent
equal value
God's
action
verbally
nourish
communicates
romance
trustworthy
understand
prays
considers
listens
divine
Christ's
initiative
spiritual

DAD
(Session 11)
manager
minister
model
manage
prayerfully
shepherds
needs
model
transfer

**RESOLVING CONFLICT—
COMMUNICATION III**
(Session 12)
anatomy
confront
forgiveness
stuffing
blowing
expectations
hurt
weapon
controlled
intensity
love
carefully
prayer
seek
grant
impossible
attitude
action
choice
trust
initiative
resist

**THE POWER OF
BLESSING—
COMMUNICATION IV**
(Session 13)
oneness
insult for insult
meaning to hurt by action
or word
unforgiving
heart
rights
feelings
responding kindly when
offended
forgiveness
Word
blessing
life
walk

**LEAVING A LEGACY OF
DESTINY**
(Session 14)
(no blanks to complete)